MINDFUL MANAGEMENT

MINDFUL MANAGEMENT

HOW ENTREPRENEURS SHOULD USE THE POWER OF MEDITATION TO SUCCEED

WILLIAM LOWRIE

NEW DEGREE PRESS

COPYRIGHT © 2019 WILLIAM LOWRIE

MINDFUL MANAGEMENT

How Entrepreneurs Should Use the Power of Meditation to Succeed

ISBN   978-1-64137-248-0   *Paperback*

        978-1-64137-249-7   *Ebook*

CONTENTS

INTRODUCTION

—

Weeks after I graduated high school, I was sitting in my house and received a call. It was my father.

"Will, I don't know how to say this, but Brian is dead."

I was eighteen when my brother died.

He overdosed.

I broke into what felt like an endless stream of tears.

I hopped in the car with tears flowing down my face and turned on the radio. It was 2015, yet the 2009 hit *Dynamite* by Taio Cruz started blasting. I was in middle school when the song came out, but I vividly remember those summer days, when my brother and I would be playing video games to that exact song.

* * *

"According to the National Institute of Health, 58% more college students scored higher on a narcissism scale in 2009 than in 1982," wrote Joel Stein in the May 2013 edition of *Time Magazine*. *"Millennials got so many participation trophies growing up that a recent study showed that 40% believe they should be promoted every two years, regardless of performance. They are fame-obsessed: three times as many middle school girls want to grow up to be a personal assistant to a famous person as want to be a senator...Their development is stunted: more people ages 18 to 29 live with their parents than with a spouse."*[1]

The *Time* article was aptly named *"Millennials: The Me Me Me Generation."*

This article backed up its claims with plenty of data, research, and statistics.

The evidence didn't make the article easier to stomach, being one of the 'trashed' individuals described. Although I would

---

1   (Stein, 2013)

like to refute a lot of these assertions and point out a lot of this generation's strengths, I won't do that.

Instead — like a true millennial would — I'm going to tell you a different story about what the article and statistics are really showing:

The majority of my generation wants to be entrepreneurs.

More explicitly, in 2018 Ernst and Young surveyed 1,200 millennials and found that 58% of millennials report that they have considered starting their own business.[2]

We certainly have the opportunity to become entrepreneurs.

Today's entrepreneurship is glamorous, just think of Mark Zuckerberg or Bill Gates. They took a chance and won big! Both these iconic figures, and many more, are enjoying the fame and fortune that resulted from their risk-taking; they are special. This is why many millennials, including myself, admire them.

Why can't I be special?

Why can't I be an entrepreneur?

---

2   (EY.com, 2019)

This dreaming has cultivated a new wave of what we call "wantrepreneurs." People who dream of being an entrepreneur, but are not willing to put in the long hours it takes to become one.

The current image of entrepreneurs is flying private jets, flaunting fortune, and having lots of leisure time.

However, this is as far from the reality as possible. Being an entrepreneur is about working around the clock and dedicating your life to your craft. The success of your company is completely dependent on your efforts. If you want free time, work a 9am-5pm job. If you want fortune, work for an established company with strong cash flows. If you want fame, use social media to build an international following. If any or all three of these are your main goals when attempting to be an entrepreneur, you will find it harder to succeed. If you simply want to be your own boss and not have to listen to others, you are not going to find it in entrepreneurship. You will still have to listen to your investors, your clients, your business partners, and many more. If you want to be an entrepreneur, enjoy the process and the unique moments you will experience along the way. It doesn't need to be your passion, but you have to appreciate it or you will burnout and likely fail.

Despite how negative these statements sound, don't be misled. This book is certainly *not* trying to steer you away from starting your own business or, if you already have one, trying to get you to quit.

In all honesty, it is a reality check.

According to the most recent data from the Bureau of Labor Statistics, about 70% of businesses fail within the first ten years.[3]

Being an entrepreneur is a grueling, challenging, wearing process on your mind and body.

My fear is that too many of my peers may quit before they reap the rewards of entrepreneurship. Perhaps they haven't been prepared, or they didn't know the risks, or they weren't ready financially, or perhaps it was simply too difficult.

If entrepreneurship is one of the most difficult business and personal endeavors one can take, how do we make sure we — the emerging generation of aspiring entrepreneurs-- are ready?

We start with our minds.

---

3   (Bls.gov, 2019)

* * *

This is where meditation comes into play.

Meditation has started to become a lot more mainstream in recent decades, but is still skeptically viewed.

How can sitting in silence for a couple minutes a day be life changing? How can it change the mind? The most common excuse I hear is, *"I don't have 20 minutes to spare each day. I am too busy."*

As you will soon discover, this is nonsense. Not being able to dedicate a couple minutes a day to your mental health is like saying you can't eat healthy because that food doesn't taste good. Just as you can find healthy food that you like, you can find a couple minutes a day to meditate. Think about the time that you spend checking social media, watching videos, playing games, or drinking. If none of those situations apply, by the end of this book you will realize that in the long run 20 minutes of meditation is much more beneficial than having even 20 extra minutes of sleep each day.

"But William, being an entrepreneur has nothing to do with meditation. Why would I waste 20 minutes on meditation, when I could use those 20 minutes to work?"

Wow, you nailed the topic of this book right on the head, but let me provide a reason why I am writing this.

We live in a stress-idolizing culture where it is glamorous to brag about how busy or overwhelmed one is. I can't tell you how many times a person has complained to me about their list of tasks to complete, and I would barely acknowledge that and start reciting my stresses.

Personally, I used to view stress as a necessary evil. If I ever wanted to achieve anything, I would have to grind through the long, stressful hours of work. Now I understand that my previous assumptions couldn't be farther from the truth. In fact, as I will explain in more detail later, stress inhibits the ability to make good decisions. Consider for a moment: When was the last time you made a good decision while stressed? I would guess it's pretty hard to think of a moment. So, how do we reduce stress and focus on our problems or stresses at the same time? It seems like the two are mutually exclusive, but this book will be a guide to showing that it is possible to have the best of both worlds, especially in entrepreneurship.

What jolted me to write this book was my personal experience. If you are not a believer in meditation, you are not alone. I was like you; I always doubted meditation. In fact, I even would tease one of my closest friends who has been practicing meditation for years. But one day I gave it a shot.

At the time, I was working at a major corporation and frankly I wasn't surrounded by a lot of my friends. Most were at college or working elsewhere in the world and it was tough to keep in touch. I became lonely and started putting in longer hours and used work as a release from that loneliness, which resulted in added anxiety and stress. Then I decided to try meditation to give myself some peace-of-mind. The results were staggering. First, I actually started to enjoy silence, which was weird for an extrovert like me. But then, I started to see changes in my work results. I simply became a better employee who was more productive and learned faster. But the most surprising thing was I wasn't as stressed as I had previously been. Meditation created "headspace" and allowed me to do more while expending less energy. Seeing this empirical evidence that meditation can directly impact your performance in the workplace, I wanted to write a book to share my knowledge.

Thus, I started interviewing entrepreneurs including Thor Cheyne (the founder and CEO of Medallion Wealth Advisors), and Sanjib Kalita (a serial entrepreneur who is currently the co-founder and CEO of Guppy). In addition, I interviewed experienced meditators and advocates such as Andrew Feinstein (the author of *Find Your Mind*).

* * *

Years removed from my brother Brian's death, I still have that hot summer day engraved in my mind like it was yesterday.

Dynamite by Taio Cruz still rings, the smell still lingers, the memory still plays. For those who have lost a loved one, I'm sure you can relate. However, I want to focus in on my mindset for the months directly after.

I didn't seek help. Instead, I acted as though everything was fine and started my college career. Quickly, I resorted to alcohol and other vices to cope with my stress, and I didn't perform to my standards in school. Worst of all, I actively tried to bring others down.

In retrospect, I had imprisoned myself within my own misery and as the saying goes, *"misery enjoys company."* Internally, I was broken and it directly impacted me externally. It wasn't until I started meditating and rebuilding myself from within that I was able to fully heal and flourish externally.

The same goes for businesses: in order to succeed as innovators, they need to build from the inside out. This rebuilding starts internally with your mindset.

* * *

This has led me to my theory:

Most people believe businesses fail because of outside forces — markets and customers.

But what if I told you that nearly every successful startup founder I've interviewed or researched shared that business failures were more often caused from within? In fact, research shows us that 13% of failures are due to a loss of focus.

Founders who are unable to control their minds and harness the power of their mindset tend to fail.

Founders who control their minds and harness the power of their mindset find a way to succeed. Therefore, I am convinced we can dramatically increase the chance of startup success by having more founders learn to meditate and harness the power of their minds.

Meditation has the ability to physically change the structure of your brain and how you think. Logically, let's break down the problem into its most fundamental pieces and rebuild the solution:

- I want to change my results. How do I do that?

- I change my actions. But how do I do that?

- I change my thoughts or mind. Where do I start?

Changing your brain can change your thought process and how you see problems. In this book, I am going to reveal how cultivating the mind through meditation can drastically influence the way individuals approach business obstacles.

* * *

This book, as a whole, explores the intersection of meditation and entrepreneurship. I'll examine how harnessing the power of our mind can help develop four core principles of an innovator's mindset:

- Intention

- Creativity

- Cognition

- Perseverance

Furthermore, I will show how the developed mindset can help you face obstacles such as:

- Dealing With Failure

- Low Energy Levels

- Lack of focusing on the Long Game

- Declining Well-Being

At the core of these eight points is the firm belief that the innovator's success is driven primarily by internal rather than external forces.

As you read on, you will discover stories, insights, and lessons from experts in entrepreneurship and meditation including:

- How John Paul DeJoria, the founder of John Paul Mitchell and Patrón Spirits, endured homelessness twice in an effort to build his businesses

- Research that has shown that the mind has the ability to heal - or harm - the body

- How Russell Brand, a British comedian and actor, used meditation to overcome his addictions

* * *

On the surface, this book is targeted towards entrepreneurs or aspiring entrepreneurs. However, I use entrepreneurship as a means to show the powerful effects of meditation. The title, *Mindful Management*, refers to two things: managing a business with the right mindset and managing your mind and well-being. Subsequently, the lessons throughout this book can be useful to anyone, especially within the workplace.

Ultimately, there are plenty of stimuli in this world that can distract you. However, by meditating and by focusing on each task at hand, this book can be your proof that 20 minutes a day of focusing on yourself and your mental health can improve your life substantially.

PART 1

THE LANDSCAPE

CHAPTER 1

THE EXCITEMENT OF ENTREPRENEURSHIP

———

"My first job was an ice cream scooper in a store called Magoo's Ice Cream Parlor," detailed Kevin O'Leary, a renowned businessman who is most recognized for his appearances on *Shark Tank* and his popular alias "Mr. Wonderful."[4]

"The very first day I got there, I was scooping ice cream and at the end of the day, we were closing the store at six o'clock, and the woman who owned it said, 'Listen, I want you to get down on your knees and scrape all the gum out of the Mexican tiles.'... And I said, 'Wait a minute. I'm not a scraper, I'm a scooper.' She said, 'No, no, you are going to do whatever I say, I own this store.

———

4   (Inc.com, n.d.)

Scrap the gum.' And I said, 'I'm not doing it.' And she fired me. It was so humiliating. I realized that there are two different places in business: people who own businesses and people who work for people that own businesses. I determined that day that I wanted to be the person that owned the business, because I never wanted to be put in a place where I couldn't control my own destiny. Years rolled by and I realized that that was a crucial moment for me and I owed her a huge debt of gratitude." — Kevin O'Leary[5]

* * *

Entrepreneurship is exciting.

In this era, there are more opportunities than ever to make money. You can create YouTube videos, sell products through dropshipping, or do affiliate advertising. No wonder entrepreneurship is now being depicted as glamorous. It is glamorous, but probably not for the reasons you are thinking of. Entrepreneurship is becoming more and more mainstream and accessible; the question is whether you want to put the effort in.

Entrepreneurship is hard work. If it were easy, everyone would do it. Entrepreneurship is filled with daily obstacles and constant criticism, but in return, you obtain the excitement of building something. Your business may have social purposes.

---

5   Ibid.

Your business may be built around your passion. Your business may solve huge problems and make other people's lives better. There is an endless list of what your business can be. Most importantly, all startups have the potential to yield happiness, excitement, and purpose. All of the responsibility is on you, the owner. This might sound scary to some, but for entrepreneurs, this challenge is exhilarating. This will, in all likelihood, lead to a rollercoaster of emotions, but thriving in uncertainty will lead to continuous opportunities to improve and learn.

There are a multitude of reasons why entrepreneurship is so exciting, but I want to highlight three:

- Perpetual Learning
- Decision-Making
- Problem Solving

* * *

PERPETUAL LEARNING:

"There's a rule of life that says you're either growing or you're dying," said Lou Holtz, a former football player, coach, and analyst.[6] His words are a bit harsh, but hold some truth.

---

6   ("Lou Holtz On The Secret To Leadership" 2015)

Entrepreneurship is filled with roadblocks. However, simply stopping cannot be an option. Entrepreneurs try to find ways over, under, around, or through. They do this through learning. If you don't know how to do something, you learn how. Alternatively, if you don't learn how to do it, you learn to hire and lead someone who can. If you don't do either, how can you build your business?

At the age of 13, Gary Vaynerchuk was fascinated by the popularity of baseball cards, and he believed that he could make money trading them. His dad lent him $1,000 to buy baseball cards and, as Gary puts it, *"I blew it. The best part of the story is, I went to Costco, Price Club at the time, and bought a bunch of boxes of a non-good year, non-good sets, because I was just too excited. It was burning a hole in my pocket. I pretty much burnt that thousand."*[7]

However, Gary was determined to make this work. Therefore, he started reading the Beckett baseball card guide everyday for as long as he could and set up tables at baseball card shows. Gary detailed his experiences: *"I would get there at 6:00 or 7:00 am. The show would open at 9:00 am, and I would have my table and I would sit there for hours and I would [move each card's position on my table] and I would always come around and try to understand it from [the consumer's] perspective... I'm*

---

7   (Freeman 2011)

thinking about, 'what would you have to see [at my competitor's table] that would then make [my table] stand out.'"[8]

Despite not knowing the terms, Gary was doing industry and competitor research and learning as much as possible. He obviously made mistakes, but later reflected and learned from them, which allowed him to reach a point in which he was earning *"$2,000 - $3,000 a weekend."*[9]

* * *

DECISION-MAKING:

Effective and efficient decision-making is at the core of entrepreneurship.

On a daily basis, entrepreneurs will make decisions that will affect the business, from the initial concept and branding to growth and goal setting. Some decisions are more influential than others, but each allow the entrepreneur to decide exactly how the business will look.

The ultimate business will be heavily influenced on a series of decisions.

---

8   (GaryVee 2016)
9   (Vaynerchuk 2013)

As a high school math teacher in 1993, Paul Carney saw the first web browser in NCSA Mosaic. Carney recalled his initial reaction, *"'That is awesome. What is this thing called the web? I've got to figure out what this thing is.'"* He was fascinated and so he gave himself a challenge: *"build a business using the web. In 1997, I launched the business and looked around and was like, 'What can I do?'"*

At this time, there wasn't a lot on the web yet, therefore Carney didn't have a lot of guidance. However, Carney was determined to complete the challenge and explained, *"My wife was a pharmacist and she put together these baskets for people that had all the necessities that new moms wouldn't think of having and I looked at it and was like, 'What a great idea! I can make a basket business out of that.' So, that's what I did."*

Carney decided that he would fulfill all the orders on his own and set up his suppliers. Carney detailed, *"I lined up vendors that I got my supplies from. I had a local pharmacy that gave me a discount. I could add to their orders for pharmacy based goods and then I would purchase it at a 10% premium above wholesale price. In addition, there is a company in Boston called The First Years and they tend to make a lot of baby products like nasal syringes and baby clippers. I reached out to them and showed them my business plan and asked them for a $1,000 credit line to order from them and, surprisingly, they gave it to me. They shipped me truckloads of stuff, so the minute I got that invoice, I paid them and I never had a problem. I went back to them 6* *months later and asked them for a $5,000 credit line and there was no issue, because I had a reputation of paying my bills."*

To Carney's surprise, his basket business was growing at an alarming rate and he couldn't keep the fulfillment process running while also working a full-time job. Carney continued, *"I had to choose. I either had to do this or that. So, I gave up both. I didn't start this company to be in the baby basket business, so I found a national retailer and sold it off. I then joined a friend and started another company called TechHound, which ultimately sold to Techies.com."*

Decision-making vastly influenced the structure of Carney's business. He decided what his product would look like, how he would fulfill it, and ultimately whether he'd continue to operate the baby baskets business.

* * *

PROBLEM SOLVING:

Businesses are built around solving a problem. Amazon simplified online buying and selling. Netflix popularized on-demand streaming media. Uber and Lyft created more accessible transport. In fact, problem solving is probably the most important aspect of entrepreneurship. Entrepreneurs are responsible for identifying and solving problems from investors, customers, employees, and others. Ultimately, your ability to solve problems can help change lives.

As graduate students at Stanford University, Larry Page and Sergey Brin created BackRub, a search engine that indexed pages around the school's intranet and made them searchable for users. The search engine received immediate praise from Stanford students, leading to the idea of creating a search engine that would help the world efficiently access information. Page and Brin named their new search engine Google. *"Google's mission is to organize the world's information and make it universally accessible and useful...That's a very broad mission... we are not going to achieve it any time soon... it is almost an impossible task. But, it's an exciting task and one that you can get other people excited about and they can help you,"* said Page.[10] Page's and Brin's desire to solve problems and continuously develop Google's software revolutionized and continues to change the internet.

* * *

These are just a few of the exciting opportunities that you experience with entrepreneurship. There are plenty more that draw people to the field. However, 70% of startups fail. Subsequently, there is an innate risk when it comes to starting your own venture. This risk is only enhanced when one is unfamiliar with the misconceptions about the industry.

---

10   (Corporate Valley 2013)

CHAPTER 2

MISCONCEPTIONS

—

The typical depiction of entrepreneurship is that you get to set your own work hours, you get to be your own boss, and you get a chance to make lots of money, which could lead to fame. What is there not to like? Well, this idealization of entrepreneurship has led to the rise of "wantrapreneurs."

"Wantrapreneurs" are people who dream of being an entrepreneur, but are not willing to put in the long hours it takes to be one. They focus on their external image and enjoy detailing to friends and family about their future success rather than actually working towards it.

"Wantrapreneurs" are more likely to fail because they don't have the right mindset when it comes to starting a business and think that the venture will be easy.

In reality, as previously stated, entrepreneurship is hard work and exciting; unlike popular depictions of entrepreneurs, entrepreneurship isn't a "get rich quick scheme." Businesses and brands aren't created overnight. It takes consistent and relentless dedication each and every day to build it.

CB Insights, a market research company, conducted a survey of 101 failed startups asking them "What are the reasons startups fail?" When posed this question, most of the post-mortem startups identified multiple reasons for their failure. Some of the findings from the survey include the following:[11]

- 42% of post-mortem startups failed because there was no market need for their services or products

- 19% of post-mortem startups failed because they were out-competed

- 13% of post-mortem startups failed because they lost focus

- 9% of post-mortem startups failed because they lacked passion

---

11   ("The Top 20 Reasons Startups Fail" 2018)

These reasons for failure can be consolidated into three common misconceptions when entering entrepreneurship:

1. The Right Idea is Everything

2. Entrepreneurship is an Easy Way to Get Rich

3. Overnight Successes are Common

* * *

MISCONCEPTION #1:
THE RIGHT IDEA IS EVERYTHING

A great idea can lead to quick success in the entrepreneurial world, however this is the vast minority. There are too many variables that you cannot fully predict until you launch your venture. To start, there is competition. As the barriers to entering most industries are lowering, competition is increasing at an alarming rate. Therefore, it is imperative to differentiate your business and become unique. You might believe that you have a distinctiveness to your business or product that sets you apart from the competition, but the customers will be the ultimate determinant of that. That brings us to the second aspect: the customers and the market demand. The customers are the most important part of a startup. Without customers, your business doesn't exist. Therefore, focus on customer needs is a top priority and, in most cases, your first idea isn't the idea that best satisfies the customers, which implies that one must pivot.

Pivoting is something most successful businesses face in their lifetime. Pivoting is when a company changes the focus of its business to find the right customer, value proposition, or positioning. Extreme competition or little demand are indications that a business ought to pivot. Pivoting, if done correctly, can turn an unprofitable business successful relatively quickly.

For example, Netflix effectively pivoted to online streaming. In 2000, Reed Hastings approached Blockbuster CEO John Antioco and asked for $50 million for the company he founded – Netflix.[12]

Blockbuster was founded in 1985. It provided movie and video game rental services primarily through traditional brick-and-mortar stores. The company became a multibillion-dollar business with a global brand. At its height in 2004, the company had over 9,000 stores and employed 60,000 people.[13]

---

12   (Chong 2015)
13   (Harress 2013)

Netflix was founded in 1997. At this point in time, video rental stores such as Blockbuster dominated the home entertainment market. However, Reed Hastings, the co-founder of Netflix, was frustrated about the exorbitant late fees. Thus, Hastings and his fellow co-founder, Marc Rudolph, started a DVD-by-mail rental service called Netflix. Customers could rent DVDs that were shipped their homes. The business took off, but was irrelevant compared to Blockbuster.

In the aforementioned meeting in 2000, *"Reed had the chutzpah to propose to [Blockbuster] that we (Netflix) run their brand online and that they run [our] brand in the stores and they just about laughed us out of their office. Initially, they thought we were a very small niche business,"* said Barry McCarthy, Netflix's CFO at the time.[14] After this, Blockbuster clung to their business model, which relied on charging late fees. On the other hand, Netflix changed to a subscription-based service and pivoted to online streaming and original content creation. This has led to a current market capitalization of over $150 billion.[15] However, Blockbuster failed to adjust to the changing consumer needs and filed for bankruptcy in 2010.[16]

14　(The Unofficial Stanford Blog 2008)
15　("Netflix, Inc." 2019)
16　(Satell 2014)

Both Blockbuster and Netflix initially had similar ideas: to offer video rentals to consumers. However, Blockbuster's unwillingness to pivot led to their downfall as they were outcompeted and had no market need, resulting in bankruptcy. Netflix's creativity and cognition in changing their business structure allowed them to grow into one of the largest companies in the world.

* * *

MISCONCEPTION #2:
ENTREPRENEURSHIP IS AN EASY WAY TO GET RICH

It is true that entrepreneurship is a way to build wealth. However, it is not easy. You will need to invest significant resources in your business, including both time and money.

In fact, when making money quick is your motivation, instead of helping others, you increase your chances of failure. Entrepreneurship is a journey and a craft that you continuously work on mastering. Therefore, when money is the driving force, what will one do when the venture isn't going as well as planned? In all likelihood, one will become frustrated and give up because his only purpose was to make money. Without a bigger focus, staying motivated is a challenge in and of itself.

In addition, if you are simply looking to make money, you are going to burnout before the business starts to materialize. There needs to be an innate excitement when it comes to your business.

Jumpstart was launched in 2018 to offer a new type of natural disaster insurance that offers immediate payout initiated via text message. Specifically, the startup connects the insured person to the insurer. However, its existence is remarkable.

Founder and CEO Kate Stillwell detailed:[17]

My worst moment was eight days before Jumpstart's initial planned launch. We had built up a team of eight people. For 16 months, we had worked shoulder-to-shoulder with our reinsurance partner, in preparation to sign the agreement that would authorize us to start selling policies on their behalf.

But someone got cold feet, and up to $100 million – the entire pot of money we had in capital reserves to pay out our customers – was at stake.

My phone rang, and since I recognized the number calling was our partner's account manager, I excused myself and walked into the common space.

---

17   (Stillwell 2018)

I remember [the account manager] saying that he wished he wasn't the one who had to give me the news but that it had been decided that our two companies were no longer going to be working together. They had called off the partnership.

There we were: no launch, team gone, out of money, no basis of raising money. I was angry, humiliated and just plain sad. But I was still optimistic: We had fallen off the proverbial cliff, but we didn't die.

Five weeks after that initial call, me and two of my remaining teammates – people who knew their jobs would likely be gone soon – took a huge risk. We decided to spend the company's remaining funds on a flashy publicity stunt at an insurance conference in Las Vegas. We bought a "shake trailer" – which simulates an earthquake – and 400 conference attendees took a ride in it. One of them called it "brilliant marketing" and the "most fun thing" at the conference. About eight months later, his company would end up being our next partners.

But that was months away. On the afternoon of the conference's second day, I had to sit down with both team members who had accompanied me. I remember telling them, "I can't pay you after today. I have to lay you both off." One of them burst into tears.

It took us over a year to make a comeback, but we survived by the grace of a few industry insiders who provided enough funding to tide us over.

Stillwell had to deal with months of extreme uncertainty. However, her passion for her product allowed her to focus and persevere, leading to the unlikely comeback.

If you are starting a business, because you're looking solely for monetary gains or you want to be famous, you are probably going to fail. However, if you have an exciting idea and are truly passionate about delivering value to customers then you have an attitude that can improve your business further. Everything starts with your mindset and how you approach *your* business.

* * *

MISCONCEPTION #3: OVERNIGHT SUCCESSES ARE COMMON

Overnight successes are myths. The portrait of the successful entrepreneur is usually of someone whose business was an instant success. This is a dangerous vision because it can lead to frustration and loss of focus if you don't succeed quickly. In reality it takes months, and often years, of hard work and focus in order to build a sustainable, successful business.

Within the first year of a startup, the founder will, in all likelihood, experience more failure and rejection than success.

The misconception of overnight successes is best explained with a story about Picasso, the famed Spanish painter. A man once approached Picasso, pulled a napkin from his pocket, and said, *"Could you sketch something for me? I'll pay you for it. Name your price."*

The book *Creating the Vital Organization* tells the rest of the story well:[18]

Picasso took a charcoal pencil from his pocket made a rapid sketch of a goat. It took only a few strokes, yet was unmistakably a Picasso. The man reached out for the napkin, but Picasso did not hand it over. "You owe me $100,000," he said.

The man was outraged. "$100,000? Why? That took you no more than 30 seconds to draw!"

Picasso crumpled up the napkin and stuffed it into his jacket pocket. "You are wrong," he said, dismissing the man. "It took me 40 years."

---

18   (Brooks and Saltzman 2016)

The progress one makes is an accumulation of dedicated years of learning. For most, these years were accompanied by failures and disappointments which ultimately manifested into successes.

John Paul DeJoria faced homelessness twice in his life before he ultimately succeeded at building a business.

After he graduated high school, DeJoria didn't have strong enough grades to earn a scholarship for college so he joined the navy.[19] After two years, he returned, got married, and had a son. However, his wife left him and took one of the cars. Within twenty-four hours, DeJoria found out that she hadn't been paying rent and he and his son were evicted from their home. This is how DeJoria found himself as a homeless, single parent who was picking up discarded bottles to cash in at grocery stores so that he and his son could survive. The two were living out of a car and DeJoria started looking for jobs. He worked as a janitor and a truck driver, just to name a few odd jobs he took on. However, DeJoria claims that he learned the most from his experience as an encyclopedia salesman. DeJoria explained the experience, *"I would just go out there and bang on doors - the average encyclopedia sales-man that was on commission lasted three days after training. I was out there about three and a half years and made pretty*

---

19   (Smith 2017)

good money. The company would tell us, 'When the going's tough, the tough get going, and never give up. You must knock on door number 100 as enthusiastically as you did on the first door that was closed in your face.'[20]

DeJoria had found a stable source of income and was able to get his family into a house.

Eventually, DeJoria left his sales job for a manager position at *Time Magazine*. However, he left after the boss told him that without a college degree it would take him nine years to be promoted to the position of vice president. He subsequently worked for a couple other companies, but was fired from all of them. DeJoria then decided to start his own business and detailed, *"After I was fired for the third time, I started a consulting firm in 1978. For a couple years I did that. it was tough. But it was still my own business. Then I knew I wanted to find my niche. I wanted to be an owner of a business that did something physical. That's when I started John Paul Mitchell Systems with [Paul Mitchell] who was a super hairdresser."*[21]

DeJoria and Mitchell had lined up an investor with $500,000 to back their salon products business.[22] However, the deal fell through. DeJoria recalled, *"The guy backed out. And we*

---

20 (Feloni 2015)
21 (Feloni 2015)
22 (Smith 2017)

didn't have another option. Inflation in the US was over 12%, interest rates 17% - it was a terrible time. But we believed so much in what we were going to do, we were going to do it."[23]

DeJoria needed this investor's money to live, so after the man backed out DeJoria was once again homeless. *"I lived in my car, and I learned how to live off a couple of dollars a day. It taught me how to survive. I slept in my car, and I could shower by the pool at Griffith Park. I'd go to the Freeway Cafe in LA after 9 in the morning, because for 99 cents you got one egg, one piece of toast, one orange juice or coffee, and either one piece of bacon or sausage. Then I'd go to a Mexican restaurant called El Torido between 4:30 and 5:30 in the afternoon because for 99 cents you got a margarita and some food like little tacos or chicken wings. I explained my situation to the girl who worked there after she asked, and they'd occasionally bring me an entrée,"* explained DeJoria.[24]

Despite all of the rejection and failure, DeJoria kept pushing forward and turned John Paul Mitchell Systems into a great success with an estimated annual revenue of more than one billion dollars. This success led him to his next successful venture: Patrón Spirits Co.

---

23 (Feloni 2015)
24 Ibid.

DeJoria is now estimated to have a net worth over two billion dollars.[25]

It took two experiences with homelessness and countless obstacles and failures before John Paul DeJoria found success. More specifically, John Paul Mitchell Systems wasn't initially successful, leading DeJoria to live in his car in an effort to build the business.

* * *

Entrepreneurship is exhilarating. You get to build your own business, you get to learn each and every day, and you get to influence the world. However, businesses succeed or fail based on a number of different, interacting variables. Therefore, the better informed you are about the misconceptions and hardships, the better your odds of success will be. One of the best ways to prepare is through developing mental fortitude, because your brain is arguably your most powerful tool.

---

25   ("John Paul DeJoria" 2019)

CHAPTER 3

THE BRAIN

Let's examine a problem. You have 12 people. 11 of them are all the same weight. One is either heavier or lighter than the rest but we do not know which. You have a see-saw and you can weigh the collective three times. How do you identify the uniquely-weighted person with 100% accuracy?

Spend some time and attempt the problem. You are encouraged to use the space below to work through the problem.

Did you find the correct answer?

Here's the solution:

Weigh four people on one side and four on the other.

Take three people off of the left side of the scale. Take three people off of the right side of the scale and move them to the left side. Take three people who haven't been weighed and place them on the right side of the scale. Weigh the new group of eight people

In most cases, there will be three people's weights that we are unsure of. Therefore, weigh two of these people against each other to determine the solution.

Two scenarios are detailed below:

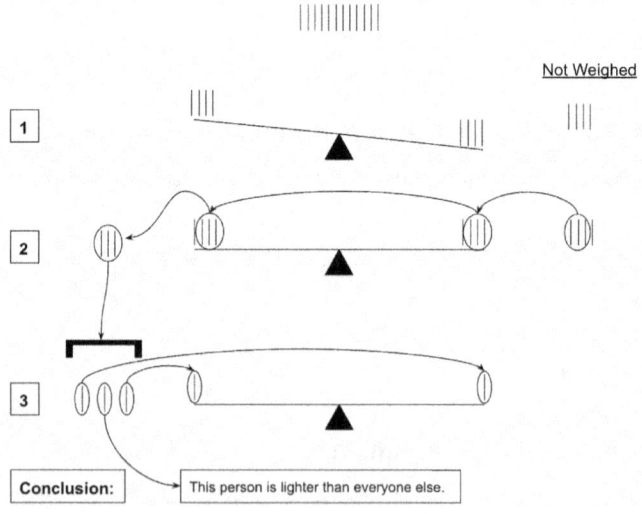

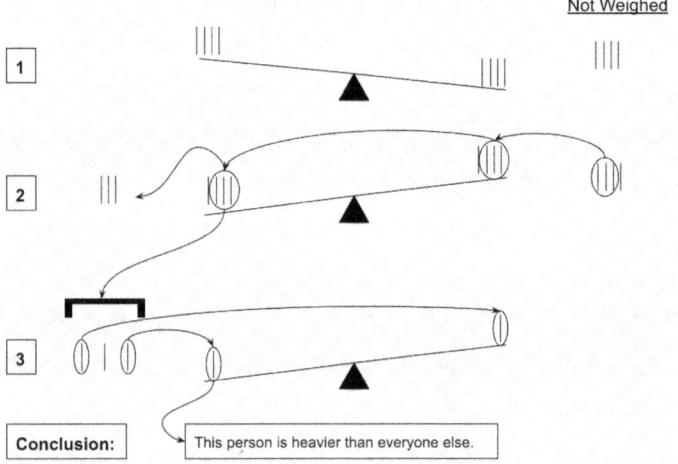

But, the more important question: Did you try more than once? Did you seriously attempt to solve the problem before looking at the answer?

The question is certainly difficult, but whether you persisted can be an indicator of whether you have a fixed mindset or a growth mindset.

The difference between the two mindsets are based on the beliefs people have about learning and intelligence. When people think that their abilities, such as intelligence, cannot change, they have what is referred to as a "fixed mindset." When people think that their qualities can grow with time, experience, and effort, they have what is called a "growth mindset."[26]

---

26   (Dweck 2015)

People with growth mindsets seek challenges and are resilient. When they encounter errors, they process it, learn from it, and correct it. This mindset also leads to increased motivation and achievement. For example, seventh graders who were taught that intelligence is malleable and shown how the brain grows with effort demonstrated a significant increase in math grades.[27]

The effects that the right mindset yielded for seventh graders is incredible, but what about entrepreneurs? Does the right mindset and brain influence success?

The short answer is yes, but let's take a deep dive into the brain.

The brain is incredibly powerful. According to *The Age of Spiritual Machines*, author Raymond Kurzweil estimated that the human brain is capable of twenty million calculations per second, most of which are done subconsciously.[28] These subconscious and conscious calculations influence your thoughts and ultimately influence your actions.

Therefore, if you could strengthen your mind and mindset, you can change your actions and results. In entrepreneurship, a strengthened mind could imply better understanding of the obstacles ahead and thus a greater chance of success.

---

27 (Dweck 2008)
28 (Kurzweil 2000)

To observe the power of the mind, let's develop a basic understanding of how the brain works.

Below you will find a breakdown of the brain.[29]

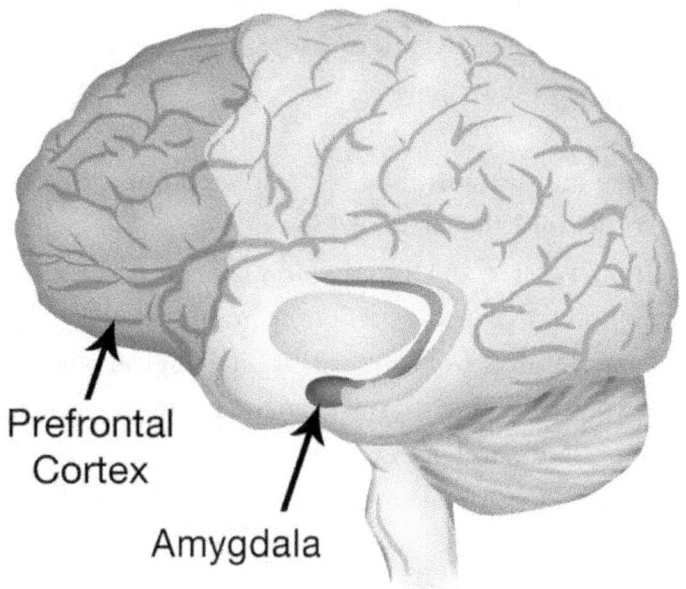

Prefrontal
Cortex

Amygdala

The brain is a very complex organ, but I will only focus on the amygdala, prefrontal cortex, and insulae. To start, the amygdala is the alarm system of the brain. It is located in the middle of the brain and is responsible for many of our initial emotional responses and reactions, including the "fight-or-flight" response. The amygdala is specifically

29   ("Katieringley.Co", n.d.)

related to anxiety, fear, and stress. If the brain perceives something as dangerous or extremely stressful, the amygdala will release cortisol, a stress hormone that aims to regulate the body but can often times make you more stressed. Cortisol can lead to a perpetual loop of stress as the amygdala gives way to cortisol and cortisol reinforces the amygdala's reactions.

Moving on, the prefrontal cortex is split into three distinct sections: the lateral prefrontal cortex, the medial prefrontal cortex, and the orbitofrontal cortex. The lateral prefrontal cortex is the part of the brain that allows you to look at things from a more rational, logical, and balanced perspective. It's involved in modulating emotional responses and overriding automatic behaviors or habits. The medial prefrontal cortex is the part of the brain that constantly references back to you, your perspective, and your experiences. It processes information, thinks about the future, and infers other peoples' points of view. Finally, the orbitofrontal cortex involves the cognitive process of decision-making.[30]

Although all three serve very important and distinct purposes, we will refer to the collective as simply the prefrontal cortex from here on out. In summary, the

---

30   (Gladding, M.D. 2013)

prefrontal cortex as a whole allows you rationalize, view problems from different perspectives, and mediate emotional responses, all of which is especially important in decision-making.

Lastly, in each brain there are two insulae, one in the right hemisphere and one in the left. This is the part of the brain that monitors bodily sensations and is involved in experiencing "gut-level feelings." Their functions include compassion and empathy, perception, self-awareness, cognitive functioning, and interpersonal experience.[31]

There are plenty more aspects of the brain that we could discuss, but the amygdala, prefrontal cortex, and insulae are specifically important when it comes to decision-making.

In general, entrepreneurs and decision-makers want strengthened prefrontal cortices and insulae with reduced amygdalae.

Furthermore, the brain is split into two hemispheres: the left and the right.

* * *

---

31   Ibid.

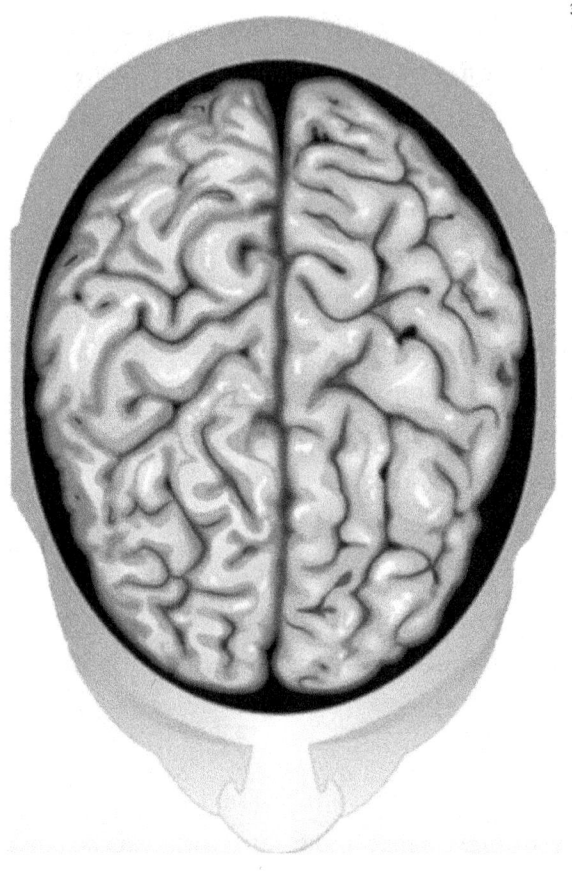

Studies have shown that there are major differences between how the brain's left and right hemispheres operate. Mainly, the left hemisphere controls the right side of the body and is responsible for language and speech. The right hemisphere

---

32   ("The Origins Of Language" 2013)

controls the left side of the body and is responsible for creativity and imagination.

The split-brain experiment showed empirical evidence of how the two hemispheres actually process information.

In the late 1900s, an outdated treatment for severe epilepsy was cutting the corpus callosum, the part of the brain that connects the two hemispheres in order to reduce the electrical activity in the brain. The treatment was effective for epilepsy, however, without the corpus callosum the right and left hemispheres could not share information with each other.

The experiment studied a handful of people who had gone through the procedure and had them focus on a black dot. A word or picture would then quickly appear to the left or right of the central dot. Anything that showed up on the right side of the dot would be processed by the brain's left hemisphere, the section that is responsible for logic, language, and speech. Therefore, the patient's answer would match the word or picture. On the other hand, anything that showed up on the left side of the dot would be processed by the right hemisphere, the section that is responsible for creativity and imagination. Thus, the patient was unable to say what they saw. However, the patient would then be asked to close his/her eyes and let the left hand draw out a picture. Like magic, they were able to draw a picture of the word or image that they had previously claimed not to have seen. In one specific trial, Dr. Michael Gazzaniga flashed two images on the screen: a hand saw on the left and a hammer on the right.

Dr. Michael Gazzaniga: *"What did you see?"*[33]

Patient: *"I saw a hammer."*

Dr. Michael Gazzaniga: *"Just close your eyes and draw with your left hand."*

The patient does as he is asked.

Dr. Michael Gazzaniga: *"What's that?"*

Patient: *"A saw?"*

Dr. Michael Gazzaniga: *"What did you see?"*

Patient: *"A hammer."*

Dr. Michael Gazzaniga: "What did you draw [a saw] for?"

Patient: *"I don't know."*

---

33 ("Split Brain Behavioral Experiments" 2007)

Amazingly, the patient thought he only saw one image but the additional drawing shows that he, in fact, saw both images. There are many implications of this study, but the director of the Institute of Cognitive and Brain Sciences at the University of California, Berkeley, Richard Ivry, breaks the study down by saying, "*The split study really showed that the two hemispheres are both very competent at most things, but provide us with two different snapshots of the world.*"[34] The two "different snapshots" or two different perspectives could be problematic in management. A major part of management is making the best decisions possible. However, the split-brain experiment shows that you could potentially decide to do two different things depending on which part of the brain is "in control."

Therefore, it is extremely important to strengthen the bond between the right and left hemisphere when it comes to decision-making. By strengthening these two centers, it helps connect logic with creativity. Integrating the two perspectives can ultimately lead to better actions and decisions.

* * *

The connection between the two hemispheres of the brain and the strength of the prefrontal cortex, amygdala, and

---

34   (Wolman 2012)

insulae are instrumental in one's decision-making. Subsequently, this information indicates the importance of one's brain structure.

However, does the brain even have the ability to change?

In the recent past, many believed that the brain did not change after childhood, but research has since shown that not to be true.

Neuroplasticity is the process by which your brain changes in response to experiences and attempting to learn new skills.[35] If you've ever changed a habit, you have experienced neuroplasticity firsthand. To best explain the idea of neuroplasticity, think of the brain as a connected power grid with billions of pathways, or roads, lighting up every time you think or do something. Some of the roads are traveled often which becomes our habits and regular ways of thinking. For every time we do a particular task or think a certain way, we strengthen the road and the road becomes easier to travel. However, if we start thinking differently or trying to learn a new skill, it is initially very hard to continue. In reality though, it is your brain changing, because the "road" is not well traveled. For example, it is the hardest to get to the gym for the first time. However, after continued practice

---

35 (Fuchs and Flügge 2014)

it becomes easier and easier to consistently exercise as a new "road" starts to form.

Neuroplasticity demonstrates that the brain can change over time. As your thoughts change, old habits and actions will slowly disappear and new ones will emerge. Therefore, by building mental fortitude and adopting a strong mindset we can change our thoughts, actions, and results, which can influence the success rate of startups.

CHAPTER 4

THE INNOVATOR'S MINDSET

"Innovation distinguishes between a leader and a follower"

- STEVE JOBS, CO-FOUNDER OF APPLE.

Innovators are risk takers. Innovators drive change. Innovators act differently, communicate differently, but most importantly think differently.

Innovators change the world.

In 1609, astronomer, physicist, and engineer Galileo built his first telescope, and the following year he discovered four new "stars" orbiting Jupiter. He published his discoveries, which also contained descriptions of the "stars" surfaces, and quickly rose to celebrity status in Italy. His findings aligned with Nicolaus Copernicus' theory, which claimed that planetary motion followed a heliocentric, or sun-centered, system.[36]

However, these findings contradicted the Aristotelian view of the universe which argued that all other planets and stars, including the sun, orbited around the Earth. In other words, the Aristotelian view claimed that Earth was the center of the universe. This view was widely accepted by both scientists and theologians.[37]

In 1616, Copernicus' argument for a heliocentric universe was placed on an index of banned books by the Catholic Church. Furthermore, Galileo was summoned by the Catholic Church and told he could no longer support Copernicus.[38]

Despite this, in 1632 Galileo published *Dialogue Concerning the Two Chief World Systems*, which outlined the debate on heliocentrism. Soon after, the Roman Inquisition convicted Galileo and put him under house arrest for once again supporting heliocentrism.[39]

---

36 (McMullin, 2007)
37 Ibid.
38 Ibid.
39 (Hilliam 2005)

Galileo displayed extreme courage by following his beliefs, especially due to the backlash from the Catholic Church and other scientists. However, Galileo's findings ultimately became scientific fact, changed our view of planetary motion, and revolutionized the field of astronomy.

Galileo was an innovator.

* * *

You can find innovators in all eras. Benjamin Franklin experimented with and learned about electricity by flying a kite during a thunderstorm. This led to his invention of the lightning rod, which helped protect houses and ships by grounding electrical currents from lightning, leaving the house or ship undamaged. The Wright brothers invented and flew the world's first successful airplane which ultimately led to a new era of transportation.

In this era, you can find innovators in all professions. However, the most common place to find them is in entrepreneurship. For instance, Larry Page and Sergey Brin revolutionized search engines by founding and developing Google.

These successes can be attributed to each individual's intelligence, but these innovators have a similar trait: their mindset. I characterize this mindset through four main facets:

1. Intentions

2. Creativity

3. Cognition

4. Perseverance

* * *

INTENTIONS:

Intentions are what motivates you. These motivations will ultimately dictate your actions. Therefore, your intentions ought to be centered around goals that are in your complete control such as excitement, because that will help you push past the tough times that entrepreneurship has to offer.

CREATIVITY:

Creativity drives innovation, because it is a differentiator in business. Specifically, 324 decision-makers from large enterprises were surveyed in 2014 and 82% of them believed that "companies that are more creative gain greater business benefits like revenue growth and market share."[40]

COGNITION:

Cognition is how we process information and store knowledge. There are a lot of cognitive processes that influence your decision-making abilities including perception, attention, memory, and reasoning. Subsequently, all of our cognitive processes must be very strong in order to reason at the highest level.

PERSEVERANCE:

Perseverance is the determination to continue to work hard. Competition is prevalent in all industries and the willingness to consistently outwork your opponents is necessary.

* * *

The innovator's mindset is especially helpful when facing common entrepreneurial challenges, such as:

1. Dealing with Failures

---

40   (Forrester Consulting 2014)

2. Lack of Energy

3. Lack of Focus on the Long Game

4. Trouble Maintaining Well-Being

DEALING WITH FAILURES:

Rejection and failure are common for entrepreneurs. In fact, 42% of post-mortem startups fail due to a lack of need in the market.[41]

However, using creativity, one can either view this "failure" as a learning opportunity or look to pivot, like Netflix.

LACK OF ENERGY:

Entrepreneurs are notorious for working long hours, which takes a considerable amount of energy. If one lacks energy, one's business will suffer, especially if the competition is energetic and working harder. This is exemplified through the fact that 19% of post-mortem startups fail because they were outcompeted.[42]

---

41 ("The Top 20 Reasons Startups Fail" 2018)
42 Ibid.

Strengthening cognition can reduce the amount of energy needed to make decisions and ultimately yield more energy in the long run.

LACK OF FOCUS ON THE LONG GAME:

When entrepreneurs view their startup as a "get rich quick" scheme, they lack patience. This lack of patience can cause frustration and yield lack of focus, which is the reason why 13% of post-mortem startups fail.[43]

To help develop patience and focus on "the long game," one can have the right intentions and persevere from the beginning. Therefore, one's end goal is always in mind, yet they are still willing to work hard every day.

TROUBLE MAINTAINING WELL-BEING:

When working long hours and focusing all one's energy on the startup, it is easy to let your well-being slip. As one's well-being slips, so does their happiness. Without happiness, what's the purpose of the venture? This loss and lack of passion is the reason why 9% of post-mortem startups fail.[44]

---

43 Ibid.
44 Ibid.

To maintain one's well-being, it is important to have some sort of workout routine for both your physical health and mental health.

* * *

The innovator's mindset can be extremely valuable, especially when approaching these common challenges listed above. However, the mindset is easier to describe than adopt. Thus, how does one adopt the innovator's mindset?

Meditation.

Meditation has the ability to help you embrace each facet of the innovator's mindset, changing your thoughts, actions, and results.

Seeing the connection between mindsets, meditation, and entrepreneurship, I have developed my theory: by adopting a daily practice of meditation, one can develop the innovator's mindset which can lead to greater startup success rates.

PART 2

THE POWER OF
THE MIND

CHAPTER 5

HOW MEDITATION AFFECTS THE BRAIN

———

Mindfulness is simply being aware and fully present. You might be asking yourself: *"I am always aware, so am I not already mindful?"*

- I would challenge this thought by questioning:

- Are you actually aware?

- Are you actually present?

- Are you thinking about that project that you need to finish?

Are you thinking about that important meeting that you are creating a presentation for?

If you are thinking about the future, then how can you truly be present? In reality, it is hard to find someone that is truly present. The only person that could make the argument that they are fully present is the Dalai Lama himself. However, it doesn't mean that the everyday individual cannot strive for complete mindfulness.

The average person has an estimated 60,000 to 80,000 thoughts a day and many of these thoughts tend to be repetitive, revealing the difficulty of being mindful.[45] We waste a lot of energy ruminating on the past and imagining future scenarios that never occur.

If we can be more mindful, we will be able to streamline our thoughts, reduce the mind's repetitive nature, and approach challenges with flexibility. One of the most effective techniques for being mindful is meditation, the practice of observing your thoughts.

* * *

---

45   (Chopra 2017)

Bob Roth is the vice president of the David Lynch Foundation, which helps teach transcendental meditation within universities, in prison and rehab centers, to veterans who suffer from post-traumatic stress disorder, and many more.

Roth uses an ocean analogy to best explain the practice of transcendental meditation, *"You're in a small boat. All of a sudden, you get these huge 40-60 foot waves and you think 'Oh my god. The whole ocean is in upheaval.' Well, not really. In reality, the ocean is a mile deep. The ocean is active on the surface, but at the depth of the ocean, it is naturally silent. The analogy is our mind. The surface of our mind is the active, thinking mind. It's like the waves on the surface of the ocean. I like to call it the 'Gotta, gotta, gotta mind.' I got to do this and I got to do that. However, there is a natural desire to have some inner calm, inner clarity, inner peace, inner happiness. Deep within all human beings is a level of the mind that is already calm, already settled, already wide awake. If it is there, then it was there yesterday, it is there right now, it will be there tomorrow. We have only lost access to it. We are stuck up on the surface, the 'Gotta, gotta, gotta level.' Transcendental meditation is a simple, natural, effortless technique to allow the active thinking mind to just settle down and to experience quieter level of thoughts and then experience what has been* called 'The Source of Thought' or the 'Transcendent' part of the mind."[46]

By quieting the *"active thinking mind,"* we move away from overwhelming and stressful thoughts and analytically approach problems with additional awareness as our brains start thinking differently.

* * *

Jerry Seinfeld, one of Bob Roth's meditation pupils, provides a tangible example of the power of meditation.

Seinfeld is a comedian and actor who is renowned for his popular 1990s sitcom, *Seinfeld*. He recalled his first meditation experience, "I do remember the very first time I [meditated] and I remember that I was up the entire night because I never felt that good before."[47] Since then, Seinfeld has continued to meditate for over forty years.

On his TV series, Seinfeld was the star of the show, the executive producer, the head writer, and was responsible for casting and editing for nine years. *"I'm a regular guy... I'm not one of these crazy people that has endless, boundless energy. I'm*

---

46 (Roth and Kaegi 2014)
47 (David Lynch Foundation 2013)

just a normal guy, but that was not a normal situation to be in. So, what I would do is every day when everybody would have lunch, I would [meditate]... and then I would eat while I was working because I had missed lunch. But, that is how I survived the nine years. It was that twenty minutes in the middle of the day that would save me," detailed Seinfeld.

One twenty minute session of meditation each day aided Seinfeld throughout the majority of his life, but in 2013, Seinfeld was convinced by Bob Roth to start meditating twice a day. With the new practice, Seinfeld saw his energy increase and stated, "I'm sixty-years old... and now I am functioning on this level that I really did not think was possible for someone my age." He explained the effect that meditation has, saying, "[Meditation] is like you have a cell phone and someone gives you the charger and you go, 'Oh, now I can keep using this thing and it will work all the time.'"

Seinfeld continued to vouch for the power of meditation, by voicing a theoretical counterargument to meditating, "'Well look I am only getting five hours of sleep as it is. I'm not going to get up earlier than that to do [meditation].'" Seinfeld defended the practice by stating, "[Meditation's] better. You'll feel better sleeping four and a half hours and doing that 20 [minutes of meditation] because that's deeper than anything you get when you're asleep."

* * *

It's hard to believe that meditation can have such profound effects. Sitting in silence for twenty minutes a day seems so simple, yet also so difficult and unproductive. However, the mind is one of the most powerful instruments at your disposal. Imagine your mind as a lawn. Without constant tending, the grass will grow high and weeds will emerge, tainting the once beautiful image. Meditation is one of the best ways to tend to your mind and keep it engaged and healthy.

Despite the above discussion of meditation, the question still stands:

Why was meditation so effective for Seinfeld and others?

The simple answer is that meditation can change the brain.

Sara Lazar, a neuroscientist at Massachusetts General Hospital and Harvard Medical School, studied the benefits of meditation and mindfulness and tested them in brain scans. Lazar compared non-meditators and meditators and found that "*long-term meditators have an increased amount of gray matter in the insula and sensory regions, the auditory and sensory cortex. Which makes sense. When you're mindful, you're paying attention to your breathing, to sounds, to the present moment experience, and shutting cognition down. It stands to reason your senses would be enhanced. We also found they had more gray matter in the frontal cortex, which is associated with working memory and executive decision making.*"[48]

The brain is composed of two parts: gray matter and white matter. Gray matter is what gives humans our information processing power, while white matter is found deeper within the brain and sends information to the gray matter. Both are important, but studies have shown that the more gray matter in certain parts of the brain, the more intelligent a person is. Lazar continued by saying that "*It's well-documented that our cortex shrinks as we get older – it's harder to figure things out and remember things. But in this one region of the prefrontal cortex, 50-year-old meditators had the same amount of gray matter as 25-year-olds.*"[49] This is a notable finding, because the prefrontal cortex is imperative in rationalizing and decision-making.

Interested in her findings, Lazar decided to test how quickly meditation could affect the brain. Lazar explained, "*We took people who'd never meditated before, and put one group through an eight-week mindfulness-based stress reduction program. We found differences in brain volume after eight weeks in five different regions in the brains of the two groups.*

---

48   (Schulte 2015)
49   Ibid.

In the group that learned meditation, we found thickening in four regions:" the posterior cingulate (*"involved in mind wandering and self relevance"*), the left hippocampus (*"assists in learning, cognition, memory, and emotional regulation"*), the temporo parietal junction (*"associated with perspective taking, empathy and compassion"*), and the Pons (*"where a lot of regulatory neurotransmitters are produced"*).[50] In addition, Lazar found that the amygdala in the meditators got smaller. This is significant because, as previously explained, the amygdala is the "fight-or-flight" part of the brain and is important for anxiety, fear, and stress.

In this study Lazar was able to show that, with just eight weeks of meditation, people can change their minds. As she explains, *"Mindfulness is just like exercise. It's a form of mental exercise, really. And just as exercise increases health, helps us handle stress better and promotes longevity, meditation purports to confer some of those same benefits."*[51]

Although you can see the physical effects of meditation in your brain as early as eight weeks, the benefits continue to grow the longer you meditate.

---

50 (Schulte 2015)
51 Ibid.

In 2018, a study was published exploring brain activity in non-meditators, new meditators, and long-term meditators. The participants, individually, viewed and labeled photos as emotionally positive, negative, or neutral while undergoing magnetic resonance imaging (MRI) on their brains. Both long-term meditators and new meditators had reduced activity in the amygdala when they viewed emotionally-positive images. However, when shown emotionally-negative images, only long-term meditators showed a significant reduction in the amygdala.[52] *"Overall these findings are important because they show that alterations in key brain circuits associated with emotion regulation can be produced by mindfulness meditation,"* says Richard Davidson, Professor of Psychology and Psychiatry at UW-Madison, who led the work.[53] *"Some changes can occur in a relatively short time while other changes require much more practice. [The findings] are also sobering in highlighting the fact that alterations in responsivity to challenging negative images occurs only after several thousand hours of practice."*

Anecdotally, I find this to be understandable as I tend to become more emotional in emotionally-negative situations than in positive ones. For example, I tend to be more emotional when I am yelled at by a coach or boss rather than

52   (Kral et al. 2018)
53   (Spoon 2018)

when I am praised by them. Furthermore, *"The amygdala is not so much about feeling good or positive experience; it's a salience detector and helps alert us that something important is happening in our environment,"* says lead study author Tammi Kral, a graduate student in psychology at UW–Madison.[54] *"A heightened response in the amygdala is more linked to grasping or wanting something. So, it makes sense to not have as strong of a response, even in the face of positive stimuli, because equanimity is a goal."*

Bob Roth also explains some of the benefits of meditation by saying, *"Research shows that during transcendental meditation there is a strengthening of the connections between the frontal lobes and the back of the brain... Everything good about the brain depends on the connection between the front and back of the brain. Stress, you can say, takes the frontal lobes offline. That's why, does a stressed person have good judgment? Does a stressed person solve problems? Plan well? No, because the frontal lobe goes offline. Also, the connection between the two hemispheres are strengthened. All parts of the brain connect together during transcendental meditation and because of something called neuroplasticity those connections that we have in meditation last in daily life. That's why people report that they think more clearly, that they make better decisions, they solve problems better. Why students find that*

---

54   Ibid.

there grades and test scores go up. It's not magic, the brain is now optimized. The whole brain is functioning in a coherent, integrated way. In fact, there is a spreading of coherent, alpha brain waves from the back of the brain to the front of the brain. Alpha brain waves are indicative of a state of restful alertness. And that's what transcendental meditation yields, a state of restful alertness."[55]

In the end, these findings highlight that meditation has the ability to structurally change the brain. More specifically, meditation strengthens the prefrontal cortex and the insulae, reduces the amygdala, and increases the connection between all parts of the brain, especially the two hemispheres. These effects yield countless benefits including moderating stress and anxiety. With these benefits from meditation, one can harness the power of the brain, which ultimately has incredible effects on the body itself.

---

55   (Roth and Kaegi 2014)

CHAPTER 6

MIND-BODY CONNECTION

"Timmy" is one of multiple personalities that controls a patient with dissociative identity disorder (previously known as multiple personality disorder). When "Timmy" drinks orange juice he has no problem. However, when a different personality drinks orange juice, the patient breaks out in hives.[56]

Additionally, if "Timmy" drinks orange juice and the drink is still in the patient's system when a different personality prevails, the patient will break out in hives. The opposite is also true: if the patient is experiencing an allergic reaction and "Timmy" reappears, the hives will fade.

---

56 (Goleman 1988)

Such differences in the same body makes one wonder: how much can psychological states affect the body? The answer: a lot.

* * *

The mind-body connection refers to the phenomenon that thoughts, feelings, beliefs, and attitudes can positively or negatively affect our biological functioning. In other words, our minds can affect how healthy our bodies are.

Until the seventeenth century, virtually every form of medicine treated the mind and body as one. However, the Western world moved away from this idea and started viewing them as two distinct entities. This new thought process had plenty of benefits as it yielded great advancements in surgery, medicine, and much more, but it downplayed the importance of the mind and its innate ability to heal the body.

The mind-body connection pervades our everyday lives. You experience the effect when you feel "butterflies" in your stomach while feeling nervous or the "pounding" in your chest when you are overwhelmed and stressed out. In the same way, positive thoughts and emotions give way to positive feelings and actions.

Wim Hof has completed tasks that defy logic, but show the true effects of the mind-body connection. He has run a marathon in a desert without drinking any water and climbed Mount Everest in nothing but shorts. Hof said, *"You know people think I'm crazy."*[57] Even if Hof is crazy, how can he endure such unthinkable feats? He attributes his success to his breathing technique which has been coined as "The Wim Hof Method." In short, the method is a breathing technique aimed at reconnecting you with nature and allowing your mind and body to adapt to your environment.

In one specific laboratory example, Hof was injected with an endotoxin that usually makes the immune system respond with "flu-like symptoms like fever, chills and headache," according to Dr. Peter Pickkers, the leading researcher.[58] Hof did not have any of these symptoms, shocking the researchers. It appeared that Hof through his version of meditation was able to suppress his immune response, suggesting that his method could allow us to influence our own immune systems at will. Scientists thought that Hof might just be a freak of nature, so they conducted a study that compared two groups: the intervention group and the control group. The intervention group was trained for 10 days in the Wim Hof Method, while the control group was not trained. Both

---

57   (Vice 2015)
58   (Radboud University Nijmegen Medical Centre 2011)

groups were injected with the same endotoxin and the flu-like symptoms were lower in the intervention group.[59] Dr. Pickkers explained the findings, "*Normally, it is very difficult to increase your adrenaline levels by your own will. Adrenaline is released by the autonomic nervous system. And autonomic means that you cannot voluntarily influence it. So, if you walk outside and you are robbed on the street, you will have a heart rate of 160 and your blood pressure will be sky high within seconds. But, if I ask you now to increase your heart rate, you cannot do that. You cannot voluntarily modulate that. And with the techniques of Wim Hof, we showed that he was able to increase his adrenaline levels to very high concentrations, even higher than people that go bungee jumping for the first time. That was something that we didn't think possible before that.*"[60]

Hof built on Dr. Pickkers analysis by saying, "[When you start using the method], *you will be able to go deeper into the system and learn to control the immune system, the cardio-vascular system, the hormonal system, the muscular system, autonomic nervous system. All that, I mean, it's just learning to go back into the inner power which we all have.*"[61] Being able to specifically control the immune system could have some serious implications. As Dr. Pickkers explains, "*There are many diseases that are influenced by your immune system.*

---

59   (Kox et al. 2014)
60   (Vice 2015)
61   Ibid.

And you can imagine that it would be of interest if you could modulate that immune system response and suppress it, that it might be of benefit for patients with diseases like that." Hof believes that this method can not only suppress diseases but also aid in recovery from depression.

* * *

Hof's method of breathing is not the only way one can control the body. Tibetan Monks have long used a meditation technique called tummo. Dr. Herbert Benson of the Harvard Medical School studied three Tibetan monks to see the effects of meditation on the body's metabolism and said, *"What we found with respect to their oxygen consumption in simple meditation, they decrease their metabolism upwards of 64% and this was the largest decrease in oxygen consumption that was ever recorded in experiments by a simple restful procedure."*[62] Metabolism is the process of converting the food you eat into energy. Therefore, a lower metabolism implies that your body will burn less calories, which can be beneficial in conserving energy. Dr. Benson continued to explain the results by saying, *"What we found in these monks in very cold environments of 40 degrees Fahrenheit and wrapping themselves in wet sheets, these monks astoundingly could increase their skin temperature enough to get the sheets steaming and*

---

62 (History.com 2011)

dry the sheets. You and I would go into uncontrollable shiver-
ing and perhaps even die of too low blood pressure. They were
quite comfortable there simply by performing their tummo
meditation."[63] By meditating and focusing on their minds,
these Tibetan monks were able to lower their metabolism
and significantly increase their skin temperature.

Ultimately, the studies on the Wim Hof method and tummo
meditation are still at the forefront of science, but on the
surface they show that there is a connection between the
mind and the body. Therefore, learning to control the mind
can have lasting impacts on the health and performance of
your body.

* * *

Furthermore, thoughts carry vibrations that impact your
biochemical, cellular, and overall physiological state.[64] This
is important, because the body is made up of atoms and
water that are in a constant state of motion, which can be
influenced by vibrations. Thus, thoughts influence how atoms
function. This implies that positive thoughts will cause different physical changes in the body than negative, sad, and
pessimistic thoughts and emotions.[65]

---

63 (History.com 2011)
64 (Gough 1999)
65 (McCraty, Atkinson and Tomasino, B.A. 2003)

In practice, this is understandable. When you are happy, you tend to be energized and when you are sad, you tend to be lethargic.

With that being said, however, repressing emotions is not the aim. Studies have shown that people who repress their emotions are more likely to have disruptions in the normal balance of the stress hormone cortisol compared to people who freely express emotion.[66]

To avoid the buildup of toxic emotions, you need to remain present and aware. Paying attention allows you to identify emotions as they arise, process them, and choose how you react. One way to effectively express, feel, and purge your feelings is to talk about them. Another valuable mind-body practice is meditation, which will keep you present and allow you to modulate emotional responses.

Ultimately, the mind-body connection indicates that the mind can have a direct impact on the body and its performance. More explicitly, the mind has the ability to heal - or harm - the body. Therefore, cultivating the mind is important to any healthy lifestyle.

---

66 (Chapman et al. 2013)

CHAPTER 7

PLACEBO EFFECT

———

The remarkable effects of the mind-body connection are best seen with the placebo effect.

Merriam-Webster defines a placebo as *"an inert or innocuous substance used especially in controlled experiments testing the efficacy of another substance (such as a drug)."*[67]

The placebo effect is a phenomenon where a patient reports improvement after taking a placebo. Since the placebo has no physical properties that would aid the patient, the improvement is attributed to the patient's belief in the placebo.

---

67   ("Definition Of PLACEBO" 2019)

There is an abundance of examples and studies that have examined the placebo effect and its incredible results.

THE VANISHING TUMORS:

In 1957, Mr. Wright was suffering from advanced cancer of the lymph nodes.[68] The tumors were the size of oranges and he was given only days to live. His doctor described him as *"febrile, gasping for air,* [and] *completely bedridden."*

Then, Mr. Wright overheard people talking about a newly dis-covered horse serum, Krebiozen, which was being tested in his hospital. This new serum appeared to be effective against cancer. Therefore, Mr. Wright begged his doctor for a dose and his doctor, although doubting the drug would help, gave him an injection. A couple days passed and Mr. Wright, for the first time in months, was able to stand and walk out of his room. When the doctor returned, he found Mr. Wright joking with the nurses. X-rays showed that the tumors *"had melted like snowballs on a hot stove,"* according to the doctor. Within 10 days, Mr. Wright was discharged from the hospital.

Two months later, however, Mr. Wright read medical reports that Krebiozen was a non-effective remedy. Mr. Wright had an almost immediate relapse and the tumors returned. His

---

68   (Dispenza 2014)

doctor then told him a lie, which would currently be impermissible. The doctor told Mr. Wright not to believe the newspaper reports and that the tumor returned because he was injected with a weak form of Krebiozen. Then, the doctor injected him with what he described as *"a new super-refined, double-strength"* version of the drug. The injection, however, was pure water. Despite this, the tumors once again disappeared.

Mr. Wright continued with life until two months later when he read an American Medical Association report that confidently declared that Krebiozen was worthless. Mr. Wright relapsed and within two days he was dead.

Was the doctor wrong? Was the tumor less malignant than initially thought? Or, did Mr. Wright's belief in Krebiozen save his life for a couple extra months?

SHAM KNEE SURGERY?:

Orthopedic surgeon Bruce Moseley, then of the Baylor College of Medicine and one of Houston's leading experts in orthopedic sports medicine, completed a trial in 2002 that looked at surgeries with 180 patients.[69] All of the patients had osteoarthritis of the knee and had not undergone

---

69 (Dispenza 2014)

arthroscopy of the knee two years prior to the study. Osteoarthritis, a degenerative joint disease, has common symptoms that include pain, stiffness, and swelling.

The study was designed to look at arthroscopic knee surgery, which is a minimally invasive surgical procedure on the knee where the arthroscope is inserted into the joint through a small incision. Participants were randomly assigned to receive one of three surgeries: a debridement, lavage, or placebo. A debridement is when the surgeon scrapes cartilage off the joint. A lavage is when the surgeon uses high-pressured water to flush out the cartilage. Lastly, a placebo surgery is when the surgeon would slice through the skin to make an incision and then sew it back together. No procedure on the knee would be performed and no cartilage would be removed. Before undergoing surgery, participants were aware that they would potentially receive no surgery and wrote in their chart, *"On entering this study, I realize that I may receive only placebo surgery. I further realize that this means that I will not have surgery on my knee joint. This placebo surgery will not benefit my knee arthritis."*

After all of the surgeries had been performed, Dr. Moseley tracked the patients and their progress for 2 years. During this time, patients in all three groups reported improvements in pain and functionality. However, Dr. Moseley found that at no point did either of the intervention groups report less pain or better function than the placebo group.

In one specific instance, Sylvester Colligan, a 76-year-old World War II veteran from Beaumont, Texas, was assigned to the placebo group. After the studies, he found out that he was in the placebo group and his surgery consisted of only shallow incisions. However, after two years, he has no pain in his knee and can mow his yard again. *"The surgery was two years ago and the knee never has bothered me since. It's just like my other knee now,"* explained Colligan.[70]

Did the placebo patients' knees actually get better? Or did the placebo patients build up better pain tolerance? Did they simply trick their mind? Is it possible to heal the body through a change in mindset?

SUPERPOWERS OF CAFFEINE:

Can believing you are consuming something have the same influence as actually taking it?

Professor Dr. Irving Kirsch of Harvard Medical School tested this theory when it came to coffee. *"People report all types of effects. They get jittery, they are able to concentrate better,*

---

70   (Talbot 2000)

they become more alert. Some of these effects are clearly effects of caffeine, but, I thought, perhaps some of them are effects of thinking that you've taken caffeine."[71] Therefore, he designed an experiment that would test performance before and after the participant was given the caffeine-free drink.

"First thing that we did was to give [the participants] *a test of cognitive abilities and motor skills. We asked people, then, what they thought would happen to their ability to do these tests* [after consuming coffee]." Thus, Professor Kirsch was able to measure what the participants thought the caffeine would be able to do.

At this point, the participants completed their baseline tasks. These tasks tested the volunteers' coordination, concentration, reactiveness, and accuracy. Continuing the experiment, Kirsch explains how *"We went through the whole ritual of brewing the coffee. We had a recognized brand of regular coffee. Although what was really in it was decaffeinated coffee."*

After consuming decaffeinated coffee, the participants waited fifteen minutes before being re-measured on the various tasks. Ultimately, there was a significant correlation between what people believed the effects of caffeine to be and what

---

71   (Placebo Effect - Caffeine Experiment 2012)

the effects of the unknowingly decaffeinated coffee were. The belief of something ultimately led to a different outcome.

Does caffeine actually have the effects of better focus and alertness? Or, is it the simple taste and warmth of a hot cup of coffee? Did the participants get better at the tests through simple practice? Or is it the expectancy of certain outcomes that led to their new performances?

CHANGING THE MIND TO IMPROVE DEPRESSION:

There was a patient named Janis Schonfeld, a 46-year-old interior designer, who had suffered from clinical depression for the majority of her life.[72] At this time, however, it had worsened and she had been dealing with thoughts of suicide. Therefore, she was thrilled when she read a newspaper ad in 1997 testing a new antidepressant. The UCLA Neuropsychiatric Institute was conducting the study and was looking for subjects for a drug trial to test venlafaxine.

Schonfeld went into the office and a technician hooked her up to an electroencephalograph (EEG) to monitor and record her brain-wave activity for about 45 minutes. After that, Schonfeld left with a bottle of pills. Although Schonfeld knew that there were two types of bottles, one with the drug

---

72   (Dispenza 2014)

and one with sugar pills, but she did not know which one she had received. In fact, no one would know which type of pills she had until the end of the study, not even the doctors.

Schonfeld returned every week for eight weeks and was continuously tested. She would have to answer questions about how she was feeling and sit through more EEGs. Surprisingly, after years of suffering Schonfeld started feeling better when taking the pills. She also started to feel nauseous, but that was a good sign because nausea was one of the side effects of the drug. Due to her improving condition and her nauseous symptoms, Schonfeld was convinced she had received a bottle with pills of venlafaxine. Having observed her momentous improvements in just a few weeks, her nurse was also convinced that Schonfeld had received the drug.

At the end of the eight weeks, Schonfeld felt like an entirely new person and was no longer suicidal. Her doctor soon told her some alarming news: Schonfeld had been in the placebo group throughout the study. She was convinced that the doctor had made a mistake and asked the doctor to check the records again. The doctor checked and told her that she was given sugar pills, not the antidepressant. Schonfeld couldn't comprehend the effects. Her doctor assured her, however, that although she didn't receive the drug, it didn't mean that she hadn't made improvements. It only implied that what was making her feel better was not related to venlafaxine.

Ultimately, the results showed that 38% of the placebo group felt better, compared to 52% of the group who received the antidepressant. However, there was a more interesting discovery. The patients like Schonfeld who had improved on the placebos hadn't just imagined feeling better; they had actually changed their brain-wave patterns. The prefrontal cortex is part of the brain that contributes to personality development and, typically in depressed patients, has very low activity. The EEG recordings taken in the study showed a significant increase in activity in the prefrontal cortex in patients such as Schonfeld.

How was Schonfeld's brain able to physically change without an effective stimulant? Did she trick herself into feeling better? Or, did her belief in the remedy lead to the vanishing of her depression?

* * *

Individually, these observations can be countered or disregarded. However, for all of these cases, recovery or improvement started with their mindsets: Mr. Wright believed in the drug, Sylvester Colligan believed in the surgery, etcetera. Thus, the trend of these examples and studies have led me to believe that the placebo effect is real, reaffirming the power of the mind-body connection and the importance of tending the mind.

The placebo effect also emphasizes the importance of mindset and suggests that changing your mindset can significantly affect your outcomes or results. Additionally, with the knowledge that meditation can change our brains, we can reason that meditation could help change our mindsets and ultimately our results too.

PART 3
THE INNOVATOR'S MINDSET

CHAPTER 8

A FOUNDER'S MEDITATION

—

At this point, you might already be convinced that tending to the mind is important and you want to start being mindful. Or, maybe you are still skeptical. Regardless of your current views, I would like for you to try. I want you to feel and see the empirical evidence. I can speak about and explain the benefits of meditation, but it isn't until you actually start meditating that you will experience the benefits.

It all starts with five mindful minutes of meditation.

So let's start right now with help from Andrew Feinstein, the author of *Find Your Mind* and the creator of the YouTube series *Fifty Seconds to Find Your Mind*:

Step 1: Find a place where it is quiet and you will not be disturbed for five minutes.

Step 2: Sit up straight and place your feet flat on the ground.

Step 3: Take out your phone, navigate to its camera, and hover over the QR Code below.

Step 4: There should be a on-screen notification at the top of your screen. Click that button.

Step 5: This will take you to a guided meditation video. Click the play button and start meditating!

(Please note: If the on-screen notification doesn't appear the first time, take your finger and click on the QR Code on your phone)

Did you do it? Did you meditate for five minutes? I am very serious about this. If you didn't, I hope you will flip the page and actually take part in the exercise.

After meditating, how do you feel? Do you feel more relaxed? Are you more aware of your thoughts?

Maybe you don't feel much different, but that ought to be expected since, for a lot of the readers, it was probably your first time meditating. However, I encourage you to stick with it. To help jump-start your journey, Feinstein has created two more meditations. Schedule five minutes for the next two days and return back to this page for the QR Codes.

After you complete these three meditations, I encourage you to continue and practice. There are a variety of ways to do this, but my favorite is the mobile application called *Headspace*.

There are also plenty of YouTube videos on guided meditations that you can use.

Eventually, you will become confident enough to meditate on your own. In addition, you will find that you don't necessarily need to be in a quiet area. I have meditated in parks, ubers, and crowded living rooms. I've even meditated in a club before. The practice of meditation is simply about finding your mind, which can be done in almost any scenario.

* * *

At this point, I have communicated a lot of important information, but I hope you are convinced that the brain has the ability to structurally change and that actions are influenced by your thoughts. One way to structurally change the brain, and thus your thoughts, is through meditation. The effect of changing your thoughts and beliefs is best explained by Mahatma Gandhi:

"Your beliefs become your thoughts.

Your thoughts become your words.

Your words become your actions.

You actions become your habits.

Your habits become your values.

Your values become your destiny." — Mahatma Gandhi, Indian political and spiritual leader[73]

Therefore, in order to achieve your desired destiny, or what I will refer to as "results" or "outcomes," you must develop "the right mindset."

"The right mindset" is a very unique thing. "The right mindset" for me will look a lot different than yours, because it depends on your thoughts, which are inherently personal. "The right mindset" will also vary across cultures and industries. Therefore, you must reflect on your own life to determine what you desire most. If you desire money, you might look for the highest paying jobs. If you value family, you might look for companies that encourage a strong work-life balance. I tend to believe that if you are an innovator or an entrepreneur, you have an achievement-oriented mindset. With the innovator's mindset, there are four main attributes:

- Intentions

- Creativity

- Cognition

---

73   (Gandhi, n.d.)

- Perseverance

As I will explain, these four areas can be enhanced through daily practice of meditation.

CHAPTER 9

DEVELOPING INTENTION

———

"I. All that we are is the result of what we have thought: it is founded on our thoughts, it is made up of our thoughts. If a man speaks or acts with an evil thought, pain follows him, as the wheel follows the foot of the ox that draws the carriage.

II. All that we are is the result of what we have thought: it is founded on our thoughts, it is made up of our thoughts. If a man speaks or acts with a pure thought, happiness follows him, like a shadow that never leaves him."

— BUDDHA[74]

———

74   (Muller 2014)

One's intention when starting a business is important as thoughts dictate your actions.

To better explain this, let's examine the Law of Attraction. The Law of Attraction can be defined as: *"I attract to my life whatever I give my attention, energy and focus to, whether positive or negative."*[75] In other words, positive thoughts tend to attract positive results and negative thoughts tend to attract negative results.

For example, one study compared self-esteem and life satisfaction and found a positive correlation between the two variables.[76] To measure each participant's self-esteem, the researchers used Rosenberg's Self-Esteem Scale (RSE). The RSE includes a series of statements and participants must respond whether or not they strongly agree, agree, disagree, or strongly disagree with each statement. Such statements include "I feel that I have a number of good qualities" and "I feel I do not have much to be proud of." I would characterize the ten statements in the RSE as either positive or negative statements. Therefore, within this study, self-esteem is simply being measured by how positively you think of yourself. Subsequently, positive thinking is also correlated with life satisfaction.

---

75   (Losier 2007)
76   (Błachnio, Przepiorka and Pantic 2016)

These studies suggest that the right intentions and thoughts can influence self-esteem, life satisfaction, and results. However, what are the right intentions?

The right intentions include goals that are within your complete control. For instance, excitement is a good intention as you solely influence this. An entrepreneur can have the goal of making money, however, when this is one's main intention, one can lose motivation if one is not making money. On the other hand, if excitement is one's main intention, one will continue to work despite the circumstances.

* * *

"Every day I feel like jumping up and down at least once and crying at least once. Every day is quite a roller-coaster. Whereas when I was working in the corporate job, every day was the same as the last," explains Sanjib Kalita, the co-founder and CEO of Guppy.

As a child, Kalita grew up under eleven different roofs before graduating high school. Familiar with this change from a young age, Kalita was surprised by the repetitiveness of the corporate world. *"In the corporate world, I just sort of felt as I got promoted I sort of hated my job more and more… I wasn't excited about what I was doing and I felt like it was further removed from the situations where I am most excited and*

energized. Also, I was just not a happy person. Every morning
I get up and I would not be excited about going to work."

At this point, Kalita was approached by a friend about a
new startup that he was creating. The idea was an educational technology startup that would bring online classes
onto mobile phones through an application. *"He (his friend)*
talked to me about what he was doing in terms of trying to help
democratize education and trying to make it more accessible
to broader populations. I definitely did get excited by that and
the product. Even when I talked to other people, there was a
natural excitement and energy in my voice, which was defi-
nitely lacking with what my day job was." Therefore, Kalita left
his job, his notable position, and his good pay for less pay and
the opportunity to build something that he was excited about.
He put excitement and happiness over fortune. *"Even after*
I left, there were times where I literally had $20 in my pocket
in Manhattan and was like, 'Okay, I got to survive on this for
a week.' And even then, I was happier doing that then when
I was at my corporate job." Irynsoft, the first startup Kalita
worked for, ended up obtaining clients such as MIT, Cornell
University, and most notably, Khan Academy, a non-profit
online educational organization that provides free lectures in
the form of short videos. Since then, Kalita has continued to
work for startups, including most recently his own venture
called Guppy.

Money wasn't Kalita's main intention when entering entrepreneurship. If he prioritized money, he could have continued working at his stable corporate job. Instead he endured the emotional rollercoaster that is entrepreneurship in exchange for the excitement that comes with building and achieving.

* * *

Excitement isn't the only intention that can be used to achieve within entrepreneurship. Finding happiness is another intention that can drive you to success.

"The mindset change was around happiness. What made me unhappy...it revolved around how I determine my own values. I'm determining my own values based on the accomplishments of other people. I feel like [when transitioning] into starting your own company, you get to determine your own values," said Adrian Geddes, the founder of Alpha, Inc, an investment management company.

Geddes was a student at Georgetown University and ever since he arrived, he felt a little out of place. *"Coming to Georgetown, it's all about competition, competition, competition. And it just drove my mindset off. I just became really unhappy. People started going to these recruiting events. There [were] hundreds of people in these rooms trying to compete to see who can get the most business cards. It was just a very unhappy environment: me trying to qualify myself to someone and competing against other people."*

Despite that, he attended the recruiting events in an effort to land a coveted job. Ultimately, Geddes' hard work paid off when he achieved a job at Goldman Sachs. His peers would congratulate him, assuming it was his dream job. However, only Geddes knew it wasn't. *"I ended up being at Goldman over the summer and it just clicked: this is just not the environment for me."* He wanted to leave.

"Where it clicked was the whole process of me leaving Goldman and looking at my family heritage." In Malawi, they only have electricity from 6:00 pm - 2:00 am. *"I remember just looking at my family history: my great grandfather was the founder of a company called First Electric and the entire country was dependent on that. So, I knew somewhere in my family heritage that I could be an entrepreneur."*

First Electric was the most successful electricity company in Malawi; however, after Geddes' great grandfather died, so did the company. Therefore, as with many Malawians, Geddes and his family never had financial independence. This led to Geddes' objective to start an investment management company. *"The idea behind starting this business was to use my experiences at Georgetown to not only help my family, but also help third world countries become more financially independent."*

The first person to learn the news of his eventual departure was his roommate. *"My roommate was like, 'This is crazy, what are you doing?' He asked me two questions:"*

Roommate: *"Do you have the capital to start what you need to start?"*

Geddes: *"No."*

Roommate: *"Do you have connections to industry leaders, so you can actually start expanding?"*

Geddes: *"No."*

He had no capital and no connections, so how would he survive? Despite that, Geddes explained, *"I did it anyways. I left my job at Goldman and actually spent the rest of my summer in South Africa and Malawi. Everybody shot down the idea, but I guess that's how it usually starts."*

With the start of his new company, he was competing once again, but competing with a social purpose, which allowed him to capture his definition of happiness. Geddes reflected,

"I just couldn't see myself working so many hours and being paid. Someone else is determining what I am worth."

* * *

Meditation can help develop the right intentions such as excitement or happiness. As one meditates, one learns to modulate emotions and approach situations with no judgment, allowing one to enjoy the moment.

For example, let's examine a negative emotion such as frustration. Frustration is an emotion we have all dealt with. Think back to the last time you were stuck in traffic. In most cases, it brings an emotion of rage: Why is this happening to *me*? However, this emotion will not help you get past traffic. Traffic simply *is*. Most people view traffic as a bad thing, but who is to say what is good or bad?

To elaborate further, there is an old parable about a wise farmer. The wise farmer had one horse and used this horse to travel to the closest town ten miles away to do business. One day, the horse ran away and his neighbor came over to lament the farmer's situation.

Farmer's Neighbor: *"I heard your horse ran away! I'm so sad for you. That's bad luck."*

Farmer: *"Good luck, bad luck. It's all the same."*

A couple days later, the farmer's horse came back and brought another ten horses with him. The farmer's neighbor came to celebrate.

Farmer's Neighbor: *"Look at all these horses! This is good luck!"*

Farmer: *"Good luck, bad luck. It's all the same."*

The next day, the farmer's son was trying to tame one of the new wild horses. The son fell off the horse and broke his leg. The farmer's neighbor returned to grieve.

Farmer's Neighbor: *"Your son broke his leg. I am sorry for your bad luck."*

Farmer: *"Good luck, bad luck. It's all the same."*

The following day, a war broke out. A brigade of men came to draft all able-bodied men to fight in the war. Since the farmer's son had a broken leg, he was spared. The farmer's neighbor came to rejoice.

Farmer's Neighbor: *"Congratulations! Your son doesn't need to go to war. I know that is good luck!"*

Farmer: *"Good luck, bad luck. It's all the same."*

The story from the wise farmer exemplifies that events that are generally looked upon as bad luck can lead to good luck and vice versa. Therefore, we must accept our present moment and move forward. There is usually little reason to allow frustration or negativity to cloud your judgment, because the current moment could ultimately lead to success.

Meditation teaches the mind to stay present and to modulate emotions, promoting the right intentions. Developing these intentions can yield self-esteem, satisfaction, and motivation to continuously evolve one's startup.

CHAPTER 10

ENHANCING CREATIVITY

—

"Imagination is more important than knowledge"

- ALBERT EINSTEIN

Creativity is all about discovering new ideas. Take this book (or any book) for an example. What can you do with it? You could read it. You could fold the pages into paper airplanes. You could construct a paper mache hat. The list is endless as long as you have the imagination and creativity to think of new ideas.

Creativity in business drives innovation. *"Creativity is essential in business because it's a differentiator,"* wrote Tucker Marion, an associate professor at Northeastern University's D'Amore-McKim School of Business and director of the Master of Science in Innovation program.[77] Marion continued, *"If you're looking at an iPhone versus a Samsung, at the outset, they're very similar. But once you start digging, there's more creativity in the iPhone. Take facial recognition, for example: it's a seamless user experience. Just because someone is first to market with a feature doesn't mean they're more creative. Design and the user experience mean a lot to overall creativity of a feature or service."*

In 2014, Forrester, a market research and advisory firm, surveyed 324 decision-makers from large enterprises across the world who influence creative software purchases. Forrester found that 82% of these companies believe that *"companies that are more creative gain greater business benefits like revenue growth and market share."*[78]

This survey also found that the companies that foster creativity tend to achieve exceptional revenue growth compared to their peers. Specifically, *"58% of survey respondents that said their firms foster creativity had 2013 revenues exceeding their 2012 revenues by 10% or more. In contrast, only 20% of less creative companies performed similarly."*

Furthermore, IBM conducted a survey in May 2010 of more than 1,500 CEOs from 60 countries and 33 industries

---

77 (Landry 2017)
78 (Forrester Consulting 2014)

worldwide, and found that creativity was the most cited leadership quality needed for future business success. As Frank Kern, a senior vice president for IBM Global Business Services, said, *"Coming out of the worst economic downturn in our professional lifetimes — and facing a new normal that is distinctly different — it is remarkable that CEOs identify creativity as the number one leadership competency of the successful enterprise of the future. But, step back and think about it, and this is entirely consistent with the other top finding in our study — that the biggest challenge facing enterprises from here on will be the accelerating complexity and the velocity of a world that is operating as a massively interconnected system."*[79]

The amalgamation of these surveys and research indicate creativity's importance in growing businesses.

* * *

Creative leaders are comfortable in uncertainty and build new possibilities by constantly evolving. Take Steve Jobs, the late co-founder and CEO of Apple, for instance. Steve Jobs started Apple in his family's garage when he was twenty-one years old with his co-founder Steve Wozniak.[80] Their vision

---

79 (IBM 2010)
80 (Knappenberger 2010)

was to revolutionize computers and make them more accessible to average retail consumers.

"These computers are going to revolutionize life and I felt like, 'Oh my god, I'm a part of this huge revolution... We're talking about everybody is going to have a computer in the home and nobody in the outside world believes us,'" said Steve Wozniak, the co-founder of Apple.

Apple's first big product was the Apple II, released in 1977. It was the first highly successful, mass produced computer. Robert X. Cringely, a technology journalist and former Apple employee, recalled, *"What was revolutionary about the Apple II was its use of color, the fact that it had a built-in keyboard, and it was the first one to look like a consumer device. So, it was a huge success, you know it was an astounding success right from the beginning."*

There were many obstacles after this moment and Jobs was eventually fired for a multitude of reasons, including his lackluster performance on the Macintosh team. For the next eleven years, Jobs built another company called NeXT, which originally developed and manufactured computers that were aimed towards business markets. The computer itself didn't sell very well because of the high price point. As Alan Deutschman, author of *The Second Coming of Steve Jobs*, detailed, *"[NeXT's] software was just breathtaking."* Therefore,

NeXT started focusing on its software. In addition, Apple's operating systems and software at the time were unable to compete with Microsoft. Subsequently, Apple bought NeXT for $400 million in 1996 and Steve Jobs quickly became interim CEO of Apple.

From 1996 until 2011, Steve Jobs and Apple continued to innovate and bring products to market that had never been conceived before, including the iPod, iPhone, and iPad. Also, Apple was and continues to be incredibly successful with their line of Macintosh computers.

Jobs was able to see something no one else could perceive and achieved his original vision of making computers accessible to average Americans. This was done through consistent innovation, flexibility, and creativity. Steve Jobs explained, *"Creativity is just connecting things. When you ask creative people how they did something, they feel a little guilty because they didn't really do it, they just saw something. It seemed obvious to them after a while. That's because they were able to connect experiences they've had and synthesize new things. And the reason they were able to do that was that they've had more experiences or they have thought more about their experiences than other people. Unfortunately, that's too rare a commodity. A lot of people in our industry haven't had very diverse experiences. So they don't have enough dots to connect, and they end up with very linear solutions without a broad perspective on the problem. The broader one's understanding of the human experience, the better design we will have."*

* * *

Research and Steve Jobs both demonstrate that creativity is valued in business, but can creativity be learned? Or is it something you are born with?

In the 1960s, the deputy director from NASA approached George Land, a former consultant and general systems scientist, and said, *"Look, we have a lot of people working for us. We need some way to select the people that are the most creative so they can go on the teams that are facing the toughest problems. Can you give us some kind of an instrument or test that we can give to find those people?"*[81] Land created an effective test that helped NASA identify the most creative workers.

After developing the test, Land wondered if creativity was genetic or if it could be learned.

Therefore, *"[My team and I] created a sample of the American population with 1,600 children and started it out when they were about five years old,"* said Land. He gave these children the same test that he had given to NASA employees.

---

81   (Tedx Talks 2011)

He re-tested these same children when they had turned ten years old, then again when they were fifteen.

The results found that the proportion of people who scored at the "Genius Level" of creativity were:

- 98% amongst 5 year olds

- 30% amongst 10 year olds

- 12% amongst 15 year olds

- 2% amongst 280,000 adults (average age of 31)

The rate at which people become less creative as they age is quite astonishing.

Land explained the findings: *"What we found from the studies with children and looking at the way brains work... there are two kinds of thinking that occur in the brain and they use different parts of the brain and it's a totally different paradigm in the sense of how we form something in our minds. One is called divergent. That's imagination. That's generating new possibilities. The other is called convergent and that's where you're making a judgment... One is like an accelerator (divergent thinking) and the other one is like a brake (convergent thinking)."*

Furthermore, Land looked at what was happening inside the brain itself and noticed that with convergent thinking *"you find that neurons are fighting each other and actually diminishing the power of the brain, because we are constantly judging, criticizing, etc."* Therefore, as Land writes in his book *Breaking Point and Beyond*, *"What we have concluded is that non-creative behavior is learned."*

If non-creative behavior can be learned, then creative behavior can be learned with practice. Land challenged his listeners to develop their creativity by saying, *"Tomorrow, do an exercise. Pick up a table fork, turn your 'five year old' on and come up with 25 or 30 ideas on how to improve that table fork."*

I will challenge you to increase your creativity through meditation.

In 2014, a study examined if integrative body-mind training (IBMT) could improve creativity.[82] According to the study, *"IBMT is designed to facilitate the achievement of a meditative state with a balance and optimization between mind and body, and further maintain this state to regulate emotion."* The researchers took forty healthy undergraduates without any meditation or relaxation experiences and split them into two groups: the IBMT group and the relaxation training (RT)

---

82 (Ding et al. 2014)

group. Relaxation training, according to the study, *"involves relaxing different muscle groups from the head to abdomen and forces one to concentrate on the feelings of warmth and heaviness."* In other words, both groups experienced a form of meditation, but the IBMT group incorporated mood regulation while the RT group did not.

To measure creativity, they administered the Torrence Tests of Creative Thinking (TTCT) to all the participants before and after the trainings. The TTCT involves simple tests of divergent thinking, which are scored on four criteria:

- Fluency

- Flexibility

- Originality

- Elaboration

After taking the TTCT the first time, participants completed seven consecutive days of training with thirty minutes per day.

After the week-long study was done, the researchers re-administered the TTCT. The results showed that the IBMT group improved on average by 11%, while the RT group improved by around 3%.

Through this information, the researchers concluded that *"creative performance on the divergent thinking task and emotion were better following IBMT than RT, and meditation with mood regulation effects have potential benefit to levels of creativity."* in other words, meditators significantly improved their creativity. These results explored the effects of short-term meditation, but long-term meditation also showed promising results.

One study examined the effects that long-term meditation had on the functioning of the brain's right hemisphere.[83] As previously explained, the right hemisphere is responsible for creativity and imagination. In the study, non-meditators and experienced meditators completed three tasks: a pretest, a rest period or meditation, and then a posttest. Among both groups, there were no pretest-posttest differences. With that being said, the experienced meditators were significantly better in the pretest and posttest performances. The study concluded, *"These results support the hypothesis that meditation facilitates right hemispheric functioning."*

---

83 (Pagano and Frumkin 1977)

Neither of these studies conclusive found that meditation improves creativity and more studies need to be conducted to definitely prove a causation. However, the findings above lead me to believe that meditation can improve creativity.

To elaborate on my reasoning, meditation is the practice of observing one's thoughts. This awareness allows one to be more present with one's thoughts and approach problems with additional perspectives. By approaching problems from different angles, one is able to connect thoughts and experiences; and, as Steve Jobs said, *"Creativity is just connecting things."*

CHAPTER 11

IMPROVING COGNITION

How does one learn?

One theory of learning is called the experiential learning theory (ELT), which was developed by a psychologist and educational theorist named David Kolb.[84] ELT is a circular theory of learning with the following four stages: concrete experience, reflective observation, abstract conceptualization, and active experimentation. Concrete experience is simply where the learner actually experiences something. Reflective observation is how the learner observes and reflects back on the experience. Abstract conceptualization is thinking about or analyzing, rather than using sensations as a guide. Finally, active experimentation is where the learner tests their beliefs.

---

84   (Mainemelis, Boyatzis and Kolb 2002)

In summary, we learn from experiences and how we think and reflect on our experiences ultimately has an immense impact on our beliefs and views.

How we think and reflect can be explained through cognitive processes. Specifically, cognitive processes are how our brains process information. There are multiple cognitive processes that are important when developing knowledge, but I will focus on the following four:

- Perception

- Attention

- Memory

- Reasoning

PERCEPTION:

Perception is the process for capturing information from the environment and processing it.

Perception is divided into five senses: visual, hearing, touch, smell, and taste. These senses allow us to interpret and understand our surroundings.

For instance, imagine that you are watching television and smell smoke. You could perceive that it is your friend cooking on the grill outside. Since you believe the smoke is contained and controlled, you are not worried and continue to watch television.

However, what if that perception is wrong? What if that smoke was coming from the pizza you left in the oven? Your house is soon set ablaze, which could potentially lead to some dire consequences.

This example demonstrates that there are multiple ways you can perceive situations, but sometimes your perception is wrong.

ATTENTION:

Attention is the process for selecting an object on which to concentrate.

In this information era, you choose what to pay attention to. Do you get your news from CNN, Fox News, Facebook, etcetera? Ultimately, the information that you choose to pay attention to has a strong influence on your beliefs.

For example, months before the 2008 financial crisis individuals ignored the fact that many banks were lending to homeowners with bad credit and instead steadfastly held on to the fact that the housing market had never failed. By focusing on the wrong information, they were unable to see the looming threat of a global financial collapse.

MEMORY:

Memory is the process of storing, finding, and accessing knowledge.

What is the capital of Singapore? Who was your childhood best friend? Where do you live?

You are able to answer these questions through your memory.

Many believe that memory is like a video camera, recording experiences and storing them away for recall. However, memory is generally unreliable. Think about a conversation you had with a friend, co-worker, or significant other yesterday. Can you perfectly recollect that conversation verbatim? In most cases, you can not.

Dr. Charles Brainerd, a professor of human development, explains, *"A key rule about memory change over time is what we call fade-to-gist. This is, we lose the details of experience rapidly but retain our understanding of its gist much longer. After attending a baseball game, we may quickly forget what the score was, who pitched, and what we had to eat, but not that our team won and we had a fun evening.*"[85]

REASONING:

Reasoning is the process that involves problem-solving and decision-making.

Once you have processed information through perception, attention, memory, and other cognitive processes, you use these findings to reason out your decision.

However, as I've explained, perception can be wrong, attention can lead us to focus in on red herrings rather than the important information, and memory can be unreliable.

If the information we have accumulated is wrong, we cannot trust our decisions.

Therefore, how do I ensure that my cognitive processes are focusing and concluding on the right information?

The answer is to strengthen one's cognition. One effective way to improve cognition is through meditation.

---

85   (Barclay 2013)

* * *

MEDITATION AND PERCEPTION:

One four-week study investigated the effects that regular practice of meditation had on habitual patterns of visual perception.[86] Subjects were split into three groups: a group that waited two weeks before beginning meditation, one that practiced passive relaxation for two weeks before beginning meditation, and a control group that neither relaxed nor meditated. All three groups had to undergo a specific set of tasks that included letter identification and card identification. The tasks were administered three different times, separated by two weeks.

For the letter identification task, the subject was shown a fictional word for a brief moment and would guess the number of letters. In the card identification task, the subject was shown either a congruous or incongruous playing card for a brief moment and would attempt to identify the playing card. Incongruous cards were playing cards that had the usual suit color reversed.

These tasks were designed to test whether meditation could help the subject be less influenced by habitual patterns of

---

86   (Dillbeck 1982)

visual perception. Those who meditated showed significant increases in letter identification and card identification as compared to the control group, suggesting that meditation was able to improve visual perception and allow consistent practitioners of meditation to be less influenced by their habitual patterns.

MEDITATION AND ATTENTION:

Dr. Amishi Jha, a principal investigator and neuroscientist, led a study published in 2015 to evaluate how mindfulness meditation exercises affect active-duty soldiers.[87] Jha explained, *"My research focuses on the basic mechanisms of attention, how stress depletes it and if and how mindfulness training can strengthen it. We have a tool that might benefit and protect soldiers' minds in the same way physical training intends to protect and prepare their bodies."*

Jha studied three groups of military service members. Two of the groups received meditation training while one group did not. Seventy-five soldiers stationed in Hawaii were studied, and all of them were between eight and ten months away from deployment. Both groups that received the meditation training reported being more aware of their attention. This

---

87   (Myers 2015)

helped conclude that the meditation training during pre-deployment was effective in preventing attentional lapses.

According to Jha's research, studies suggest that off-task thinking happens anywhere between thirty and fifty percent of waking hours. As Dr. Bruce West, the army's senior research scientist for mathematics, describes, *"Many military historians believe battles, even wars, have been won or lost in the warrior's mind, long before any physical conflict is initiated."* Therefore, attentional lapses could be the difference between life and death so limiting these lapses are becoming imperative. *"Soldiers are experts at standing at attention,"* according to Jha. Despite this expertise, in the midst of the physical and emotional demands of battle, maintaining exceptional attention is a far more difficult task.

Research has shown that the more mentally "fit" a person's brain is, the quicker that person is able to recover from stress, to solve complex problems, and to better handle high-demanding environments. Jha also highlights how he *"would like to emphasize that these [mindfulness] practices are powerful, but that they only work if they are exercised daily. This is why the paper was critical in finding that taking a mindfulness course that does not have a practice emphasis has essentially no benefits on attention. Similar to physical exercise, you have to do it to benefit. Only with active engagement in mindfulness exercise can attentional benefits be gained."*

MEDITATION AND MEMORY:

Dr. Dianna Quach of the California School of Professional Psychology conducted a study that examined the effectiveness of meditation on working memory capacity in adolescents.[88] The researchers split the participants into one of three groups: meditation, hatha yoga, or a waitlist control condition. All the participants had to initially take a baseline assessment that tested one's memory. Then both the meditation and the hatha yoga groups met eight times over the course of four weeks. Each session lasted for 45 minutes. At the end of the study, the participants' memories were tested again. The study stated, *"Participants in the mindfulness meditation condition showed significant improvements in WMC (working memory capacity), whereas those in the hatha yoga and waitlist control groups did not."* This study suggests that short-term meditation could have benefits in improving one's memory.

MEDITATION AND REASONING:

The amalgamation of these studies support the assertion that meditation improves cognitive processes like perception, attention, and memory. With improvement in these areas, we would expect strengthened problem-solving and decision-making skills as we have more reliable and accurate

---

88   (Quach, Jastrowski Mano and Alexander 2016)

knowledge. A study supported this assertion by stating, *"the results... indicate that participating in the [meditation group's] curriculum results in improvements in measures related to general intelligence"* and another study reported that *"the groups who learned meditation successfully solved significantly more failed problems from the pre-test session, providing direct evidence for the role of meditation in promoting insight."*[89] [90]

Meditation's ability to improve reasoning is empirically shown through Ray Dalio, the founder and former CEO of Bridgewater Associates, Ray Dalio.

"Transcendental meditation has probably been the single most important reason for whatever success I've had," said Dalio.[91] He began practicing meditation as a college student in 1969, when Maharishi Mahesh Yogi taught it to the Beatles. Since then, he founded Bridgewater Associates in 1975, authored best-selling books, and appeared on the *Time's* list of the 100 most influential people in the world. Through all of this success, he has publicly discussed his daily meditation routine as the most important reason for his achievements. Dalio describes how *"[meditation] helps slow things down so that I can act calmly, even in the face of chaos, just like a ninja in a street fight,"* and says that meditation *"gives you control over your mind."*

---

89   (Cranson et al. 1991)
90   (Ren et al. 2011)
91   (Clifford 2018)

The ability to control your mind is extremely important in Dalio's line of work: hedge funds. A hedge fund pools clients' money and invests it with the expectation to produce gains regardless of how the general markets are performing. However, investing can be very difficult due to a multitude of reasons, especially innate biases such as confirmation bias and self-attribution bias. These biases can distort opinions and lead to poor investing decisions. Therefore, a calm and rational mindset is of the utmost importance.

Furthermore, in 2008 during the height of the financial crisis and an extremely emotional time across the globe, Dalio introduced transcendental meditation to his firm. Dalio wrote, *"I [introduced transcendental meditation] because it's the greatest gift I could give anyone - it brings about equanimity, creativity, and peace."*[92] In addition, he spoke about the benefits of meditation by saying, *"When you're centered, your emotions are not hijacking you. You have the ability to think clearly, put things in their right place, and have good perspective."* Many employees began meditating regularly which was followed by some staggering results. Bridgewater Associates was one of eight hedge funds to generate gains in 2008 while the average hedge fund ended the year down almost 20%.[93] [94] Eleven years after the implementation of

92   (Feloni 2016)
93   (Barr 2010)
94   (EDHEC Business School 2009)

meditation at the firm, Bridgewater Associates has enjoyed continuous success.

Bridgewater Associates was successful before the implementation of meditation, therefore it is impossible to conclude that Bridgewater Associates is successful solely due to meditation. Despite this, the extra perspective that meditation provides likely aided employees in making rational investment decisions, especially the 2008 financial crisis.

Additionally, the military has started to see the cognitive benefits of mindfulness with their troops and have started to encourage the practice of meditation. Norwich University, located in Northfield, Vermont, was one of the first military universities to practice meditation.[95] One platoon started meditating and the results were noticeable. As Felicia Jones noted, *"I'm a senior and I've never gotten over a 3.00 [GPA]. This semester I've had 22 credits, four lab assignments, and I have a 3.60 [GPA]. I don't think I just got that much smarter, I think the transcendental meditation helps me focus, and so when I study I get more benefits out of it."* Focus wasn't the only side effect of meditating, as Mark Hagenlocher discussed that he says that *"The one thing I notice about the platoon that's practicing meditation is how the cadet leaders and the rooks are handling stress. This appears to be an effective*

---

95 (David Lynch Foundation 2012)

tool for our cadets to help them handle the stressful military school environment where they are really striving for excellence academically, militarily, and in a lot of cases physically."

In the end, the research and the empirical evidence from Dalio and Norwich University demonstrate the power that meditation can have in strengthening your cognitive processes and improving your problem-solving skills.

CHAPTER 12

PERSEVERANCE

———

"I'm convinced that about half of what separates the successful entrepreneurs from the non-successful ones is pure perseverance. It is so hard. You put so much of your life into this thing. There are such rough moments in time that I think most people give up. I don't blame them. It's really tough and it consumes your life."

- STEVE JOBS, FOUNDER OF APPLE[96]

Perseverance can be viewed as an unstoppable force. Once you achieve perseverance, the ability will give you the determination to never take "no" for an answer, and when you run into obstacles you will move past them with ease.

---

96 (Curtin 2019)

In order to achieve perseverance, one must equally value confidence, hard work, and patience:

Confidence + Hard Work + Patience = Perseverance

Confidence allows you to stay focused on your ultimate goals, while moving past small and irrelevant obstacles.

"It was within a year after I had joined Smith Barney that I knew that I needed to get into my own practice." Thor Cheyne wasn't the prototypical entrepreneur people think of. He didn't drop out of college to start his business, but instead he left a stable job at the age of fifty to start Medallion Wealth Advisers, his Wealth Management company. *"I joined Smith Barney in October 2004. I needed to get my legs under me at Smith Barney and become prepared for my departure, which came in April 2010."* As he worked at Smith Barney, he started building the infrastructure and self-confidence for his new start-up, *"I worked practically two jobs from July 2009 to April 2010 to set up the business, to create the LLC, to survey broker-dealers, to understand how to set up an RIA [Registered Investment Adviser], and to do the legal work."* When he started his own business, Cheyne described how *"It felt wonderful, the freedom and independence, and it was also overwhelming to know that I needed to generate revenue to pay my own employee. It was the first time where I was the horse and I am pulling the carriages."* The "carriages" included his

wife, children, and employees. *"They were all relying on this horse not to come up lame. There was a lot of responsibility from that perspective, but I felt great that I was independent and it was mine."*

The new ownership and responsibility led to a lot of pride. *"I did notice that when I interacted with people and they asked me about what I do, they responded differently than when I was a financial adviser working for a big company. 'Oh, you started your own business, wow.'"* Although most were impressed by Cheyne's actions, he ran into opposition. *"There were people who would say to me, 'You're starting a business when you are 50 years old with 2 kids in college. Are you crazy?' I just said, 'Maybe I am crazy, but this is what I need to do.'"* He didn't let this negativity get in the way of his progress because he had confidence in his vision. *"My personality is, if someone says something negative, listen to see if there is any fact behind it, but don't dwell on the negative, dwell on what is positive and move towards the light."* Despite the difficulties in working two jobs and facing negativity, Cheyne exhibited the confidence in himself to build a business that has had over a decade of success.

Confidence can be developed through meditation. As previously mentioned, the average person has an estimated 60,000 to 80,000 thoughts per day. This many thoughts leads to a virtually endless stream of inner dialogue, which can often end with self-doubt as one sifts through endless future possibilities. Meditation has the ability to quiet this inner dialogue and calm one's mind. Calming one's mind results in inner clarity, while quieting the inner dialogue rids the mind of self-doubt, leading to a fortified confidence.

* * *

HARD WORK:

Hard work is the next integral part of the equation. Without hard work, you will not get very far. In an era of intense competition, hard work can single-handedly lead to initial success.

"I did not know I was an entrepreneur; I was just a kid trying to make money." Jerome Smalls accidentally discovered entrepreneurship at the age of twelve. Smalls explained, *"I would wash my grandfather's car and clean out gutters for people, but then I had this idea: I could sell candy."*

At his school, there was a vending machine full of candy. *"We could only go to the vending machines during certain times of the day, especially during class and we only had five minutes between classes. So, there was limited time to get candy, and everyone wanted candy. And at the time, my mom was on EBT with food stamps."* Electronic Benefits Transfer (EBT) is a U.S. government program that gives impoverished families cash benefits to pay for food. According to the Supplemental Nutrition Assistance Program (SNAP), the average EBT payout per person is $126 per month.[97] Despite this, his mother said, *"I'm not going to continue buying you candy, but I will buy your first one."* Smalls' mother used the EBT money and bought a $13 variety pack with thirty pieces of candy. Immediately, Smalls analyzed his competition: the vending machine. *"The vending machine sells candy for $1.25, so I can just sell my candy for $1.00."* Undercutting the competition proved to be effective as Smalls explained when he said, *"It started clearing out. I went through a pack in like 2 days."* Smalls, seeing the high demand, continued, *"I realized that I needed more candy, so I tried the chocolate bar variety, but it gets hot and the bar starts melting, so I couldn't do that. I started selling chips and juice boxes too. It was a whole enterprise."* Without even knowing, Smalls was testing and analyzing different products to see which sold best.

Furthermore, he would sell candy during class, in between classes, but the best time was during his bus rides. *"All the kids from my part of town took this hour long bus ride and everybody got hungry. The bus was where I made the most money."* Smalls was making a significant amount of money, but it didn't come without obstacles, *"I got robbed in the*

---

97   ("A Quick Guide To SNAP Eligibility And Benefits" 2018)

sixth grade. *The money and the candy were gone. I felt what it feels like to lose.*" Despite the setback, Smalls continued to work hard by using every opportunity to sell candy or analyze the competition. A year later, he transferred schools and was concerned that he wouldn't have the same demand. He stated, "*I was worried that I wouldn't be able to keep the same enterprise. I wouldn't be riding the bus, but low and behold, people were still buying it like crazy. The school didn't even have vending machines, so I was the sole supplier. It got so big to the point where I was in the bathroom and I had zip lock bags full of candy that I was transferring over to my buddy to sell it for me.*" Smalls was a full fledged entrepreneur hustling to supply his school with candy.

Meditation promotes both focus and hard work. During meditation, meditators concentrate on their breath and the present moment, which helps them develop the ability to focus. In addition, since meditation reduces stress and anxiety, meditators enjoy more psychological rest, which makes work less straining and improves work ethic.

* * *

PATIENCE:

Patience plays a key role in the creative process. For instance, when creating a painting, an artist must take one's time and ensure that each stroke is purposeful. Just as an artist must be patient when completing a painting, an entrepreneur must be patient when building a business.

As previously mentioned, overnight successes are a myth. Time and effort are required before the desired results manifest. Therefore, being able to wait for success is one of the biggest lessons that many people in the current instant-gratification era must be willing to endure. As the saying goes, *"good things come to those who wait."*

Barbara Corcoran the real estate mogul exhibited this patience when building her business. She was a straight-D student in high school.[98] She had been dyslexic and had a difficult time learning anything in school. *"I've spent my entire life trying to prove once and for all that I am not stupid. That's the truth. That's what drives me,"* said Corcoran. *"I had 22 jobs before I landed the one that would make me rich. I was working as a waitress at a diner and met a man who became my boyfriend and he was the guy who said with your personality you'd be great in real estate sales."* Therefore, Corcoran took out a $1,000 loan from her then-boyfriend and they started a business in 1973. *"Within two years, I had 14 agents and a half a million dollars in sales... Five years later, my boyfriend came home and announced he was marrying*

---

98   (CNBC Prime 2018)

my secretary. I thought I would die... On the day I divided the business, my boyfriend said, 'You'll never succeed without me.'" With that extra motivation, in 1978 Corcoran committed to her craft and created the Corcoran Group, one of the first female-owned real estate firms competing against only men. *"People thought I was cute, but they didn't take me seriously. Inside I was anything but cute, I was dead serious about becoming the largest real estate broker in New York City."* However, Corcoran didn't let this become an obstacle and started to innovate the industry. *"By 1993, we were selling real estate online, two years before our competitors. I also registered all the URLs for my competitors who had a brand so that they'd have to come to me when they wanted the name. I didn't charge them for the URL. I just wanted them to call and ask for it so that I'd know when the competition started selling online."*[99] Ultimately, twenty-three years after the creation of the Corcoran Group, the company had become the largest real estate company in the city with $66 million in revenue. Corcoran's patience in building her company allowed her to persist throughout the process and helped her achieve the success that the Corcoran Group enjoys today.

One way to develop patience is through meditation.

---

99 (Eng 2019)

What is your happiest moment in life? The answer shouldn't be hard to find. The memory is usually one of the first things you think of.

For my moment, I think back to high school football. We were down 28 - 0. My team was on defense and I lined up at defensive end. With the snap of the ball, I evaded the offensive linemen and quickly met the ball carrier as he received the football. Instincts took over as all of a sudden I had my hands on the football, spun away from the ball carrier, and sprinted 60 yards the other way.

The memory seems insignificant. My team was losing and this one play would not influence the final outcome nor the rest of my life, so why did the moment make me so happy?

I was happy, because I was present. In that sprint, I didn't care about the score, I didn't care about the future, I just ran. The feeling was indescribable.

Reimagine your happiest moment. Were you thinking about the future? Did you want the moment to end? Were you worried about other people's opinions?

For most, I would expect the answers to be no, because there is a connection between being present and being happy. Subsequently, meditation promotes happiness, because meditation is centered around mindfulness or being aware and present.

The presentness and happiness that comes with meditation makes it easy to be patient as you don't contemplate on the future or your progress. Instead, meditation teaches you to simply enjoy the present and the entire process, which inherently promotes patience.

* * *

PERSEVERANCE:

The combination of these three values equates to an even more powerful value in perseverance, allowing one to approach challenges with vigor and excitement.

Jack Ma exhibits perseverance in its true essence. Ma, the founder of Alibaba, faced a lot of rejection in his life. In primary school, he failed two exams. In middle school, he failed another three. When applying to universities after high school, Ma failed three entrance exams. Although he wasn't the strongest student, he applied to Harvard ten times and was met with rejection all ten times. *"I was so bad at schooling...I tried three years for entering University and finally I got into the poorest University in my city,*" Ma explains.[100] After receiving his Bachelor's degree, Ma failed to land a job after applying to thirty different companies. Ma details one application, "*When KFC came to China, 24 people went for the job. 23 people were accepted. I was the only guy [who wasn't].*" Ma ended up working as a teacher where his pay was $10 a month. He never feared rejection, because he was confident in his abilities even when nobody else was.

In 1995, Ma visited the United States and learned about the internet for the first time. "*I searched the first word of 'beer'... I [saw] beers from Germany, beers from the USA, beers from Japan, but there's no beer from China. And, I say okay [and] type the second word 'China.' No data. Nothing... So, I talked to my friend, why [don't] I make something about China? So, we made a small very ugly looking page [about China]... It was so shocking. We launched at 9:40 in the morning. 12:30, I got a phone call from my friend. He said, 'Jack, you know you got five emails?' I said, 'What is email?'...People were so excited, [they wrote], 'where are you? This is the first time I [had seen] a Chinese website on that.*"

Ma thought this response was very interesting. Therefore, he returned to China and gathered twenty-four of his friends in his apartment. He explained that he wanted to create a

---

100 (Alibaba Group 2015)

business related to the internet. "*23 of them* [said], '*forget it. This thing will never work because there's no such thing called [the] internet in the world. You know nothing about computers, so why do you want to do this?*'" Only one out of the twenty-four showed any support when they responded, "'*Jack, if you want to try it, just try it, but if something goes wrong just come back.*'"[101] After taking a night to think about it, Ma said, "'*I still want to do it.*'" Again, the confidence that he had always exhibited as a kid still persisted when starting his revolutionary company.

Thus, Ma gathered $50,000 from eighteen founders and started Alibaba, a Chinese online commerce company.[102] There was plenty of rejection ahead though. "*I tried to borrow 3,000 US dollars from the banks. It took me 3 months but I still couldn't get it... We talked to over 30 or 40 venture capitalists. Everybody said no. Forget it...*[A] *lot of people said Alibaba is a terrible model.*" Despite all the rejection and pessimism, Ma thought, "'*I believe it. I think this thing could be big,*'" and continued to build his business. "*For the first 3 years, we did not have even $1* [of] *revenue from our business. It was not easy.*" However, he and his team continued to persevere, because customers were praising the company and saying that "'*This is such a great thing.*'"

---

101 (Alibaba Group 2017)
102 (Eternal Explorer 2019)

Ma reflected, saying, *"Little by little we built up our business. And now after 16 years, we have Alibaba group, we have Tmall group, we have Taobao group and we have Alipay. And people say, 'You are so smart, how could you make a company like that?'"*

* * *

As Jack Ma exemplified, confidence, hard work, and patience leads to unwavering dedication to one's business. Through his mindset, Ma persevered through constant criticism, doubt, and rejection, and ultimately built one of the largest businesses in the world.

PART 4

ENTREPRENEURIAL OBSTACLES

Entrepreneurship is a difficult industry filled with an abundance of obstacles. A couple of these challenges include:

- Dealing with failures
- Lack of energy
- Focusing on the long game
- Maintaining well-being

These difficulties are a large reason why 70% of startups fail within the first ten years of operations. But, by applying the innovator's mindset (intention, creativity, cognition, and perseverance) and adopting a daily practice of meditation, one can successfully face these obstacles and statistically increase their chances of entrepreneurial success.

CHAPTER 13

FAILURE

———

Failure is a necessary step towards success. Intellectually, we understand this. Emotionally, we do not. Most of us are so terrified of failing that it makes us anemic when it comes to action. We don't want to embarrass ourselves.

For example, you might have the goal of doing ten push ups in a row. Thus, you try. You get to five push-ups and on the sixth, you fall flat on your face. It is embarrassing, but now you know you must work harder to reach your goal. Ultimately, after a couple days of doing push-ups and falling flat on you face, you reach ten push-ups in a row. You succeeded! But, the success came with numerous failures and moments of falling flat on your face.

Furthermore, the fear of failure makes us more vulnerable to failing or results in performing far before our potentials. To illustrate this point, let's return to our push-up example:

Instead of continuing to strive for ten push-ups, you simply agree that five push-ups was your maximum. Therefore, everyday you simply complete five push-ups. You might eventually be able to do ten push-ups, but you would never know, because you aren't pushing yourself. Thus, although you have the ability to do ten push-ups you only put forward 50% of your potential because of your fear of failing.

This push-up example can also be applied to entrepreneurship. When faced with failure, many entrepreneurs fear other people's judgment and quit. The fear of failure may indicate why 20% of cease operations before the end of the first year.[103] Entrepreneurship, however, is filled with failures and the experience can feel like an emotional rollercoaster. Subsequently, founders need to find ways to manage this emotional rollercoaster to better deal with failure.

* * *

By adopting the innovator's mindset and focusing on creativity, one can move past failure gracefully.

---

103 (Mansfield 2019)

Creativity is simply connecting experiences and failures are some of the best experiences. There is a common quip: "*You either succeed or you learn.*" Subsequently, failure can and ought to be looked at as a learning experience.

One person who connected his experiences and leveraged his creativity was Bill Gates, one of the richest people in the world and founder of Microsoft.

Gates' first company Traf-O-Data was, in most accounts, a failure. The company read and analyzed data from road-way counters and created reports for traffic engineers. As Paul Allen, a co-founder of Traf-O-Data, recounts, "*Despite efforts to sell our wares as far afield as South America, we had virtually no customers. Traf-O-Data was a good idea with a flawed business model. It hadn't occurred to us to do any market research, and we had no idea how hard it would be to get capital commitments from municipalities. Between 1974 and 1980, Traf-O-Data totaled net losses of $3,494. We closed shop shortly thereafter.*"[104] Despite that, this failure ended up leading to Microsoft's success. Allen explains that "*While Traf-O-Data was technically a business failure, the under-standing of microprocessors we absorbed was crucial to our future success... If it hadn't been for our Traf-O-Data venture, and if it hadn't been for all that time spent on [University*

---

104 (Allen 2011)

of Washington's] computers, you could argue that Microsoft might not have happened."[105]

If Gates had given up on becoming an entrepreneur after his first failed company, Traf-O-Data, he would have never started Microsoft, which is currently one of the largest companies in the world. His ability to learn from his failed startup experience and apply the lessons to Microsoft led to his success.

* * *

42% of post-mortem startups fail because of no market need. However, with creativity, one can effectively pivot and turn a failed startup into a successful one.

Play-Doh originally began as a wall cleaner, designed to clean up the black residue that coal heaters left on walls. However, a few years later gas heaters and vinyl wallpaper became the norm and made the wall cleaner business irrelevant. The demand vanished before the company's eyes. The founders thought about stopping operation, but not before pivoting.[106]

A teacher named Kay Zufall had mentioned that people were buying Play-Doh as a material for children to make inexpensive

---

105 (Weiss 2018)
106 (Hiskey 2015)

Christmas ornaments. Zufall tried it with her students and told the company that they loved it, especially because it was cheaper and less toxic than traditional modeling clays. Play-Doh ran some market research and it got amazing reviews. Therefore, they started selling the paste and marketing it to schools. They found a demand in the market and ended up becoming one of the most successful toys of all time.[107]

Play-Doh faced becoming obsolete. However, they approached the problem with creativity and found a solution by targeting an entirely new market.

* * *

Failure is an unpleasant feeling or thought and humans tend to dislike and avoid unpleasantries. However, success is often a byproduct of failures. Therefore, how can we change our innate aversion to failure?

The answer is meditation.

As previously explained, meditation shrinks the amygdala, which is the emotional center of the brain and is responsible for stress and anxiety. Furthermore, in chapter 5, I talked about a study that looked at the brain activity in

---

107 Ibid.

non-meditators, new meditators, and long-term meditators. In this study, when shown emotionally-negative images, only long-term meditators showed a significant reduction in the amygdala. This finding suggests that when facing failure, an emotionally-negative experience, long-term meditators will be able to modulate emotions. With this modulation of emotions, one can remember that failure is a learning opportunity and can approach failure with a rational mindset.

The modulation of one's emotions often leads to the best decisions. To illustrate this point, let's revisit Ray Dalio, the founder of Bridgewater Associates and an avid meditator.

"At 12, I caddied and the stock market was hot at the time, so I would talk about stocks," Dalio explained.[108] The Links Golf Club where Dalio worked was an exclusive course where the customers included people such as the Duke of Windsor, Richard Nixon, and many Wall Street investors. With Dalio's $300 in savings, he bought Northeast Airlines, which soon merged and Dalio tripled his investment. *"So I got hooked on the markets,"* Dalio detailed.

Ultimately, this interest in the markets led to a commodity trading job, after graduating from business school in 1973. However, after two years Dalio reflected, *"That wasn't for me.*

---

108 (Business Insider 2018)

Also, at that time, people would pay me to trade the markets and I had a two-bedroom apartment and I had a roommate that moved out and I started Bridgewater."

For the first five years, Dalio enjoyed continued success and growth. *"Around 1980 or so, I had about 8 or 10 people who worked for me,"* Dalio recalled.

However, his success came to an abrupt stop. *"[Around 1980,] I thought that foreign banks had lent to emerging markets way more money than those countries would be able to pay back and we were going to have a debt crisis. And, Mexico defaulted in August 1982 and a number of countries defaulted... I figured we were going to have an economic crisis. I couldn't have been more wrong. That was the exact bottom in the stock market,"* explained Dalio. It was a big mistake, which cost Dalio more than just money. *"As a result, I had to let people go, I lost money for me, I lost money for others. I was so broke that I had to borrow $4,000 from my dad."*

Many would be deterred from the market at this point, but Dalio reflected, *"[It] was one of the best experiences that ever happened in my life, because it gave me the humility that I needed in order to balance with my audacity. I started to ask myself, 'How do I know I'm right?,' 'How do I find the smartest people I can who will disagree with me?,' 'How do I create a certain type of culture in which we bring independent*

decision makers in and we argue with each other?.' That
changed everything."

Whether Dalio recognized it at the time or not, he was promoting a culture of idea meritocracy, where the best ideas
always win out. This differed from many firms at the time
that followed an autocracy -- where the opinion of the most
senior person won -- or a democracy -- where the most popular idea won.

This meritocracy led to what Dalio describes as "thought-
ful disagreement." This term can be compared to what one
study refers to as "cognitive conflict," which is "task-oriented
disagreement arising from differences in perspective."[109]
The study found that encouraging cognitive conflicts led to
higher quality decision-making. Through Dalio's mistake, he
promoted these cognitive conflicts, which ultimately encouraged rational decision-making instead of emotional actions.

Overall, Dalio sums up his experiences well, by saying: *"The*
successes were good but they weren't my main learning expe-
rience. My main learning experience came from the mistakes
and then pausing and reflecting. I have a principle: pain plus
reflection equals progress. Pain, when we're in the moment
of pain, we tend not to reflect, but after that moment of pain,

---

109 (Amason and Sapienza 1997)

whenever anybody makes a mistake, about anything, it's not just the market, it's about life. There's a message probably there. And I believe, then if you reflect, in a quality way of what would you do differently in the future that would prevent that mistake, you'll come out with a principle." [110]

* * *

"You learn from your mistakes." The quote has immense truth. Another way to phrase the quote is that within your failures, you'll find the seeds for your success. Thus, rather than dreading failure, we need to use creativity and meditation to embrace rejection as a vehicle to get us closer to our dreams.

---

110 (Chin 2017)

CHAPTER 14

ENERGY LEVELS

The world spends billions of dollars on coffee, 5 Hour Energy, Red Bull, and other products that provide a little bit of extra energy to get through the day. However, this is simply a temporary boost. Instead, strengthened cognition and meditation have the ability to improve energy levels on a daily basis.

Many young entrepreneurs are working long hours for seven days a week in order to see their vision pan out. Therefore, energy is one of the most important resources that they need.

As Kevin O'Leary, a financial expert and star of *Shark Tank*, said, *"If I have to give one piece of advice to someone who's thinking about starting a business, I tell them this: Forget about balance. You're going to work 25 hours a day, seven days a week, forever."* Although working 25 hours a day is physically impossible, O'Leary's point is clear: *"If you want to be an entrepreneur, you have to be in 110%."* Every ounce of energy you have needs to be dedicated to building your business, because as O'Leary explains, *"You're going to be competing with people from Mumbai and Shanghai who want to kick your ass."*[111]

The competition that O'Leary refers to is a serious threat to any entrepreneur as 19% of post-mortem startups fail because of being outcompeted.[112] But, by increasing energy levels, one can outwork the competition by putting forward better quality of work.

∗ ∗ ∗

Traditionally, one rests and gains energy through sleep. However, research suggests that meditation could be more effective in resting the mind and increasing energy in the body.

Melatonin is a hormone that is necessary for a restful sleep, but stress inhibits the body's production of melatonin. The lack of melatonin causes one's body to wake up more tired than usual. Meditation, however, reduces the amygdala which diminishes stress, allowing the body to produce more melatonin and to enjoy higher quality rest.

---

111 (Berger 2018)
112 ("The Top 20 Reasons Startups Fail" 2018)

In addition, individual meditation sessions can have immense impacts on one's body. Bob Roth, the vice president of the David Lynch Foundation, explains, *"The research shows that during transcendental meditation your body gains a state of rest and relaxation in many regards, deeper than the deepest part of deep sleep. It allows the build up of stress, fatigue, tension, anxiety to be dissolved, to be eliminated. When we get to the state of deep rest, it allows the body to repair itself, there is a hormone called cortisol. Cortisol is secreted by the adrenal glands when we are anxious. When we get a good night sleep, cortisol levels drop a bit. That is why we wake up feeling fresher in the morning. Research shows that with 20 minutes of transcendental meditation, cortisol levels drop close to 30%."*[113]

Furthermore, in a 1995 study, the researchers studied twelve highly trained meditators and eleven elite runners of similar age, sex, and personality. The study found that both meditators and elite runners released a significant amount of endorphins, or hormones that provide a strong energy boost. Therefore, experienced meditators were able to achieve energy boosts through their practice.[114]

---

113 (Roth and Kaegi 2014)
114 (Harte, Eifert and Smith 1995)

With the increased levels of melatonin and endorphins and the decreased level of cortisol in one's body, meditators report needing less sleep and having more energy. One study from the University of Kentucky concluded, *"In long term meditators, multiple hours spent in meditation are associated with a significant decrease in total sleep when compared with age and sex matched controls who did not meditate."*[115]

The improved energy levels that meditation provides can be observed with Martin Scorsese. Scorsese is one of the most acclaimed movie directors of this generation and has created movies such as *Taxi Driver, Raging Bull, The King of Comedy,* and *Goodfellas.* He started meditating in 2008 and he described his overall experience by saying, *"So, for the last few years I've been practicing meditation, trying, and it's difficult to describe the effects it's had on my life. I can only mention maybe a few words: calm, clarity, a balance, and at times a recognition — and it's made a difference."*[116]

In one instance, Scorsese explained that meditation played a pivotal role in filming *Hugo.* *"In the morning, I would get up 45 minutes earlier to do meditation before I was able to face that set with children actors that can only work for like a minute, a dog that wasn't listening, Sacha Baron Cohen who was*

---

115 (Kaul et al. 2010)
116 (David Lynch Foundation 2011)

improvising everything and over-schedule and over-budget. There was only one thing I could do, calm [my mind] down and get into [meditation] and deal with the realities later." Scorsese further used meditation when directly faced with problems. *"If there is something on my mind, something I am really worried about, I just forget it and I go into meditation and somehow something comes out."*[117]

Ray Dalio explains the phenomenon that Scorsese experienced by talking about how meditation unlocks the subconscious part of your mind. Dalio said that *"the physiology of the brain is because that comes from the subconscious part of your mind that's where your inventiveness, creativity, inspiration come from, so you just go in there and somehow you come out with the answer."*

An alternative explanation for his experience is that through meditation, Scorsese was able to reduce stress levels, increase endorphin secretion, and improve his overall energy, which gave him the ability to tackle the *Hugo* set with vigor every single day.

* * *

The improved cognition through meditation can also help with the efficiency of one's work.

---

117 (David Lynch Foundation 2015)

For example, the Beatles discovered meditation in 1967 when they first met Maharishi Mahesh Yogi, a famed transcendental meditation teacher, in England.[118]

George Harrison: *"On August 24th, all of us, except Ringo, attended the lecture given by Maharishi at the Hilton Hotel. I got the tickets. I was actually after a mantra. I had got to the point where I thought I would like to meditate; I'd read about it and I knew I needed a mantra — a password to get through into the other world. And John and Paul came with me."*

Ringo Starr: *"At the time Maureen (Ringo's wife) was in the hospital having Jason, and I was visiting. I came home and put on the answerphone, and there was a message from John: 'Oh, man, we've seen this guy, and we're all going to Wales. You've got to come.' The next message was from George, saying, 'Wow, man - we've seen him. Maharishi's great!'"*

Despite their enthusiasm, the four band members did not study with Maharishi until February 1968. They traveled to India along with their wives, girlfriends, and assistants. Ringo Starr and Paul McCartney both left early due to various personal reasons and prior commitments, however John Lennon and George Harrison both stayed for seven weeks. About six weeks through the retreat, Lennon and Harrison

---

118 (Lennon et al. 2000)

appeared on the British TV talk show *The Frost Programme* and spoke about their experiences with meditation.[119]

Host David Frost: *"There were two things that Maharishi said this morning were the result for people meditating, following his system of meditation. The two things he claimed were serenity and energy. Have you found them?"*

John Lennon: *"I've got a lot more energy. It's the same energy but I don't have to tap it. The energy that I've found doing meditation has been there before - only that I could access it only during good days when everything was going well. With meditation I find that it could well be pouring down rain; it is still the same amount."*

Host David Frost: *"Is it true that any day of meditation then is equally good?"*

John Lennon: *"The worst days of meditation I have are better than the worst days I had before."*

Host David Frost: *"At the end of it - do you feel more relaxed, do you know more about yourself? Do you feel you know something more about something else?"*

---

119 (Lennon and Harrison 1967)

George Harrison: *"You don't feel like you have more knowledge or anything. You might, but it doesn't feel that way exactly. You just feel more energetic. You just come out of it and it's been refreshing."*

This dialogue gets to the core of how meditation can feel. Although the Beatles couldn't articulate why they felt a certain way, they experienced increased energy and increased happiness. Meditation increased the Beatles energy and cognition, resulting in what is regarded as the Beatles most productive period of band songwriting. In the seven weeks, Lennon detailed their progress, saying, *"We wrote about thirty new songs between us. Paul must have done about a dozen. George says he's got six, and I wrote fifteen. And look what meditation did for Ringo - after all this time he wrote his first song."*[120]

* * *

Without consistent energy and dedication, entrepreneurs will see the quality of their work decline. Therefore, energy is vital when building a business. One can use caffeine for a temporary boost, but 20 minutes of meditation a day can yield lasting energy and lasting results.

---

120 (Lennon et al. 2000)

CHAPTER 15

THE LONG GAME

———

"Most people overestimate what they can do in 1 year and underestimate what they can do in 10 years"

— BILL GATES, FOUNDER OF MICROSOFT

Overnight successes are common. Entrepreneurship is a "get rich scheme." These misconceptions about entrepreneurship make it difficult to be patient and embrace the long game.

Building a business takes time. Estimations indicate that businesses take about three years before revenue starts to significantly grow.[121] Therefore, if you are not willing to persevere for three years, then your business is statistically more likely to fail.

———

121 (Martin 2017)

Despite this estimation, 38% of small businesses ceased operations before the end of their third year, indicating that a large portion of entrepreneurs are closing their businesses before they start seeing growth.[122]

The reality is that success is a process. Every small experience, whether successful or not, culminates in the growth of a person. Therefore, consistent perseverance and dedication over the long-term are necessary to embrace the long game and enjoy the journey.

* * *

When you think of Mark Cuban, the owner of the Dallas Mavericks and founder of Broadcast.com, you might be tempted to focus on his current stature and success. However, let's examine how he entered the world of entrepreneurship.

As a boy, Cuban was in Pennsylvania trying to buy a new pair of sneakers. His dad was playing poker when Cuban asked for the shoes.[123]

---

122 (Mansfield 2019)
123 (Bloomberg 2014)

Dad: "*Those shoes on your feet look like they're working pretty well. If you want a new pair of sneaks, you need a job and you can go buy them*"

Cuban: "*Dad, I'm 12 years old, where am I gonna get a job?*"

Dad's Friend: "*I got somethin' for ya! I've got these garbage bags I need to sell. Why don't you go out there and sell these garbage bags?*"

With that, Cuban's first entrepreneurial venture was born. He decided that he would sell one hundred trash bags for six dollars, making him a three-dollar profit. "*I literally would go door to door to door: 'Hi, does your family use garbage bags?' And who could say no? So that's where I learned to sell. Every objection [I'd reply], 'Of course you use garbage bags, and I bet you pay more than six cents a piece.'*"

Using the sales techniques that he learned during his time selling garbage bags, Cuban had another idea: stamps.[124] "*I started going to stamp shows and trade shows and just working a little bit harder than other people at these shows. I would trade up from one stamp to the next. I went to a show starting with only a quarter and started with buying a single stamp. I left that show with $50 thinking, 'Hey, if I could do this, I could*

---

124 (Montag 2018)

do anything.'" After that, Cuban started to dedicate significant time to his venture. *"I spent hours sorting through the stamps."* At the age of sixteen, he became so successful that one of his neighbors gave him $5,000 to go buy stamps in New York. He reflected on the experience, saying, *"Collecting stamps is an amazing way to start to understand business. Each stamp has its own level of scarcity, of demand, of price, and as a collector you have to make decisions on when to keep a stamp, trade or sell it, and when to invest in a new stamp for your collection."* Cuban further explained that when he *"bought, sold and traded so many that the experience taught me as much about business as any class I have ever taken."*

The list of ventures continued throughout his entire life, including starting his own bar called "Motley's." Every experience throughout his life was a learning experience. Through his garbage bag business, Cuban learned how to sell. Through his stamp business, Cuban learned the dynamics of supply and demand. Every experience taught him something new. As Cuban put it, *"Never stop learning. Never stop grinding. Never stop loving every single minute of your life."* The lifelong culmination of Cuban's experiences led him to his current position as the owner of the Dallas Mavericks.

* * *

A different way to discuss the idea of embracing the long game and enjoying the journey is through the advice: strive for micro speed, but macro patience.

"Micro-speed" means that in the short-term you are consistently "doing." You are constantly working hard with the same vigor every day and throughout the day. You are looking to be as productive as possible and taking short-term actions that will eventually lead to your long-term goals. All of these actions accumulate to increasing your knowledge and mastering your craft.

"Macro-patience" means setting long-term goals that align with your values, beliefs, and desires. Instead of expecting immediate success, entrepreneurs ought to be patient and understand that reaching these goals takes time. As Malcolm Gladwell's *Outliers* explains, it takes about 10,000 hours of deliberate practice to achieve expertise.[125] Ultimately, one must be willing to trade time for both expertise and success.

One person who exemplified embracing the long game through micro-speed and macro-patience was Thomas Edison. In the late 1800s, incandescent lamps were too bright to be used for rooms of a house. Therefore, in 1878, Edison attempted to develop an improved incandescent lamp designed for household use. His idea would consist of a filament in a glass bulb. By 1879,

---

125 (Gladwell 2009)

Edison had created his first household bulb, but the product only burned for a few hours. He desired a lamp that burned for longer; thus, Edison continued to test different filaments. Edison recalled, "I tested no fewer than 6,000 vegetable growths, and ransacked the world for the most suitable filament material."[126]

Eventually, Edison tried carbonized cotton thread as the filament. Fifteen hours later, the filament finally burned out. Edison described the process, "The electric light has caused me the greatest amount of study and has required the most elaborate experiments. I was never myself discouraged, or inclined to be hopeless of success." Edison's dedication to the long process of creating a household light bulb exemplifies that greatness is often achieved after consistent commitment to an idea. Edison further explained, "Genius is one percent inspiration and ninety-nine percent perspiration."

* * *

Micro-speed and macro-patience is the combination between perseverance and intentions. These two aspects of the innovator's mindset allow one to approach each day with tenacity and patience like Thomas Edison. This unlikely combination of abilities helps one embrace the long game and inspires the necessary dedication that one needs when building a business.

---

126 ("Edison's Lightbulb" 2018)

CHAPTER 16

WELL-BEING

"Just a week before, the startup I had been working day and night on for months had utterly failed. And along with it went my sense of meaning and worth. My life was empty. Without meaning. Without purpose. I felt like there was no reason to keep on living."

— BENJAMIN FOLEY[127]

Benjamin Foley's company had failed.

Suicidal thoughts crept into his mind. Foley felt himself gradually retreating, but a shocking story rattled him to his core: *"I was voraciously reading startup blogs, I came across*

---

127 (Foley 2017)

an article about a husband/wife entrepreneurial team that had taken their own lives after their startup dream had failed. It was a heart-wrenching piece that shook me to my core and made me rethink the path I was on."

Foley learned exactly how scary the world was when he did more research on the depression, anxiety, and suicide epidemic facing startup founders and learned the following information: "*1 in 3 entrepreneurs live with depression and 30% of all entrepreneurs experience depression... Depression among entrepreneurs is much higher than depression among Americans in general, which is estimated at about 7% — although that number could be even higher due the stigma associated with discussing depression keeping people from reporting their mental illness. But at face value, these statistics suggest that entrepreneurs are four times more likely to suffer depression than everyone else.*"[128]

* * *

Psychological well-being is incredibly important in entrepreneurship as mental illness, which can be crippling to one's business and life, is a reality for startup owners. Therefore, the mental fortitude built through meditation is incredibly important on maintaining one's well-being in business.

---

128 Ibid.

Russell Brand is a great example of how the mental fortitude that meditation provides can promote well-being and change one's life.

Brand is a British comedian and actor who is renowned for his sarcastic jeers and uncanny confidence. Despite that, earlier in his career Brand was not happy as he explained that "*I used to be poor, now I'm not. And I didn't used to be famous, and now I am. And I thought that both of these significant transitions might bring a certain amount of satisfaction. They did, a bit initially.*"[129]

To fulfill his need for satisfaction, Brand looked towards drugs and became addicted, specifically to heroin. Addiction cost him jobs on television and multiple relationships with family, friends, and significant others.

Brand recalled Chip Somers, his manager at the time, acknowledging his self-destructive behavior and saying, "'*You're a complete garbage head. If you don't stop taking drugs in the next six months, you'll either be dead, in a lunatic asylum or a prison in six months time.*'"[130]

---

129 (David Lynch Foundation 2011)
130 (Ruby 2015)

The frankness got to Brand and he stopped immediately and has been drug and alcohol free ever since. However, this is not the happy ending. *"The situation got out of hand when I was clean,"* Brand continued. His addiction shifted from drugs to sex and, after that, focusing too much about other people's opinions of him. *"Drugs are just the obvious one. If someone is a crack addict or a heroin addict, they get into problems real quickly. But if you're obsessed with what other people think about you or you're obsessed with social media, it consumes your life."* In all reality, these less obvious addictions can be just as harmful. *"If you don't deal with the source, the condition will migrate and morph and attach to something else."*[131]

Brand started attacking the root problem with a twelve-step program that ultimately helped him escape his addictions. One of his foundations for recovery became meditation. *"I wanted to learn about Transcendental Meditation due to my dissatisfaction with some of the pleasures that I talked about: drugs, the fame, the celebrity, the consumerism, the wealth, all of these things that pledge happiness but deliver so little of substance,"* Brand explained.[132] Brand elaborated on his practice of meditation, *"In that meditative space I'm relieved of the constant thinking, the constant fear, the anxiety of being alive and not feeling like I'm good enough."*[133]

---

131 (Blynn 2017)
132 (Ruby 2015)
133 (Today 2017)

This realization is the demonstration of consciousness. As you become more conscious, superficial things such as *"the anxiety of...not feeling like I'm good enough"* slowly disappears. Brand explained further, *"In active addiction, I am disconnected. That is one of the defining characteristics of this condition. I look to reconnect, to recalibrate by using drugs, alcohol, technology, sex, food, domination or some other external stimulant."*[134]

This desire to reconnect is a large reason why 85% of individuals relapse and return to drug use within the year following treatment.[135] When addicted, the only way the mind is comfortable connecting with the world is through the addiction, whether that be drugs, sex, etcetera.

"I find it hard, I'm quite an erratic thinker, quite an adrenalized person, but through meditation I felt this absolute sort of beautiful serenity and selfless connection," said Brand.[136]

Brand's story speaks extreme volumes about the power of meditation. Meditation was able to not only help Brand escape addiction, but also allow him to discover happiness. For Brand, his addictions hindered his aspirations. As Brand emphasized, *"We all live in our minds and we have allowed*

---

134 (Brand 2017)
135 (Sinha 2011)
136 (David Lynch Foundation 2011)

them to become poorly tended. Meditation is a way of culti-
vating the environment in which I spend all my time."[137]

Brand's experience with meditation is not an isolated inci-
dent. Research has also explored the association between
meditation and well-being. The researchers had two groups
of thirty people, both individuals who engaged in mindfulness meditation regularly and individuals without meditation
experience. They then evaluated each person's psychological
well-being. As the study states, *"Meditators reported higher*
emotional well-being" and *"the study suggests that mindful-*
ness meditation is associated with increased psychological
well-being."[138]

* * *

Mental illness is a common problem in entrepreneurship.
Many suffer from depression, alcoholism, and many other
mental diseases, which can be crippling to one's health.
However, through the reduction of stress and anxiety and
the modulation of emotions, meditation has the ability to
strengthen one's mental fortitude and promote psychological
well-being.

---

137 (Brand 2017)
138 (Keune and Forintos 2010)

CONCLUSION

——

Entrepreneurship is a rewarding industry as you obtain the excitement of building something unique. However, it is inherently risky as 70% of startups fail within the first ten years of operations. Common reasons for startup failure include lack of need in the market, being outcompeted, aversion of failure, lack of energy, lack of focus on the long game, and trouble maintaining well-being.

To overcome these obstacles and improve entrepreneurial success rates, entrepreneurs need to develop mental fortitude and build strong mindsets. The mindset that I believe will best approach these challenges is the innovator's mindset, which is characterized through developing intention, enhancing creativity, improving cognition, and persevering.

The most efficient and effective way to develop this mindset is through meditation.

Meditation has an abundance of effects that include reducing stress and anxiety, modulating emotions, and providing more psychological rest. The combination of these effects results in better decision-making and reasoning skills, which is why I am not surprised that people such as Ray Dalio, Steve Jobs, and Russell Brand are or were avid meditators. Alec Ross, an American technology policy expert who served as Senior Advisor for Innovation to Secretary of State Hillary Clinton, has also seen this adoption of meditation in the White House, reinforcing the idea that meditation improves decision-making skills. Ross detailed, *"One of the dirty little secrets... from the White House and the chambers of power around the world [is that] a lot of the world's most powerful leaders are obsessive meditators."*[139] Subsequently, the improved decision-making skills that meditation yields, makes the practice an important tool for a person in any workplace.

Through my current assessment of entrepreneurship, mindsets, and meditation, I have reasoned that building mental fortitude and developing the innovator's mindset through meditation can result in an improved chance of entrepreneurial success.

---

139 (Koester 2018)

ACKNOWLEDGEMENTS

———

I would like to thank and acknowledge all the people who made this book possible:

My family, including David, Anne, Michael, Rachel, Mary Jean, and Dan Lowrie.

My advanced readers, who made many helpful suggestions, including Heather Gomez, Max Magid, and NeKisha Wilkins.

My illustrator, who designed the cover of *Mindful Management*, Kamakshi Bhargava.

My distinguished supporters including Clyde Shepherd, Brian Bies, and Eric Koester.

My advisors and interviewees, whose stories can be found throughout the book, including Paul Carney, Thor Cheyne, Andrew Feinstein, Adrian Geddes, Sanjib Kalita, and Jerome Smalls.

My benefactors, including Maggie Aloisio, Sagar Anne, Nick Aquino, Kwame Asiedu, Daniel Baldwin, Connor Barone, Cameron Barr, Ganzorig Batbold, Paige Bazaar, Celina Bazaar, Lance Bennett, Grant Beske, Robert Bolen, Tyler Brophy, Spencer Brown, Howard Chang, Kevin Chen, Joe Daccache, Eddie Deschapelles, Christopher Delaney, Guillermo Delso, Eric Diestelow, Phoenix Do, Craig Dsouza, Ian Erickson, Brian Ferrigno, Jeffrey Ferrigno, Adriana Fini, Bradley Galvin, Lucas Geremia, Ginger Glazer, TJ Gletner, Tristan Gorkin, Christopher Hagen, Chen Han, Donna Harris, Thomas Hawkins, Anne Herren, Alexander Hersov, Harrison Horner, Jack House, Mark Ingram, Rob Kasper, Carl Kyrillos, Ken Lawler, Ricky Lenz, Michael Leone, Lisa Liu, Jake Lyons, Zachary Magid, Braeden Mahoney, Pranav Marupudi, Lori McConaghy, Mairead O'Brien, William Ogden Moore, Zach Olson, Charlie Owen, Henry Peterson, Jake Poliner, Carter Rise, Katie Rogers, Nikki Rose, Alec Ross, Maribeth Ross, Alessandra Ruggiero, Neal Sarup, Ali Taha Brown, Kyle Taylor, Will Thacher, Ryan Toomey, Morgan Trevett, Gos Tsotetsi, Andrew Van Hoek, Cameron White, Eli Wilson, Jared Wiltshire, Ryan Young, and Patrick Yu.

Thank you to everyone else who helped me along the way.

BIBLIOGRAPHY

———

INTRODUCTION:

"Business Employment Dynamics". 2019. *Bls.Gov*. https://www.bls.gov/bdm/
us_age_naics_00_table7.txt.

Stein, Joel. 2013. "Millennials: The Me Me Me Generation". *Time*. https://time.
com/247/millennials-the-me-me-me-generation/.

"The Millennial Economy 2018 Survey". 2019. *EY.Com*. https://www.ey.com/
en_us/careers/the-millennial-economy-2018-survey.

CHAPTER 1 - THE EXCITEMENT OF ENTREPRENEURSHIP:

Corporate Valley. 2013. *Inspiring Google Story - Larry Page*. Video. https://www.
youtube.com/watch?v=f_eiMKp4QW8&t=322s.

Freeman, Mike. 2011. "How Gary Vaynerchuk Built His Empire". *Shopify*. https://
www.shopify.com.sg/blog/4072192-how-gary-vaynerchuk-built-his-empire.

GaryVee. 2016. *What Selling Baseball Cards Taught Me About Customer Attention*. Video. https://www.youtube.com/watch?v=TUPlWPJx-LY.

Inc.com. n.d. *Why Humiliation Drove Kevin O'leary To Start His Own Business.* Video. https://www.inc.com/video/why-humiliation-drove-kevin-oleary-to-start-his-own-business.html.

"Lou Holtz On The Secret To Leadership". 2015. *WSJ.* https://www.wsj.com/articles/lou-holtz-on-the-secret-to-leadership-1448302765.

Vaynerchuk, Gary. 2013. "Gary Vaynerchuk: How I Became An Entrepreneur". *Inc.Com.* https://www.inc.com/gary-vaynerchuk/how-i-became-an-entrepreneur.html.

CHAPTER 2 - MISCONCEPTIONS:

Brooks, Scott M, and Jeffrey M Saltzman. 2016. *Creating The Vital Organization.* [S.l.]: Palgrave Macmillan.

Chong, Celena. 2015. "Blockbuster's CEO Once Passed Up A Chance To Buy Netflix For Only $50 Million". *Business Insider.* https://www.businessinsider.com/blockbuster-ceo-passed-up-chance-to-buy-netflix-for-50-million-2015-7.

Feloni, Richard. 2015. "John Paul Dejoria Explains How He Went From Homeless To A Billionaire". *Business Insider Australia.* https://www.businessinsider.com.au/john-paul-dejoria-billionaire-entrepreneur-2015-4.

Harress, Christopher. 2013. "The Sad End Of Blockbuster Video: The Onetime $5 Billion Company Is Being Liquidated As Competition From Online Giants Netflix And Hulu Prove All Too Much For The Iconic Brand". *International Business Times.* https://www.ibtimes.com/sad-end-blockbuster-video-onetime-5-billion-company-being-liquidated-competition-1496962.

"John Paul Dejoria 2019 "John Paul Dejoria". 2019. *Forbes.* https://www.forbes.com/profile/john-paul-dejoria/#25a4e19424a4.

"Netflix, Inc.". 2019. *Finance.Yahoo.Com.* https://finance.yahoo.com/quote/NFLX/.

Satell, Greg. 2014. "A Look Back At Why Blockbuster Really Failed And Why It Didn't Have To". *Forbes.Com.* https://www.forbes.com/sites/gregsatell/2014/09/05/a-look-back-at-why-blockbuster-really-failed-and-why-it-didnt-have-to/#235e3a0b1d64.

Smith, Scott S. 2017. "John Paul Dejoria Rose From Homelessness To King Of Hairstyling". *Investor's Business Daily*. https://
www.investors.com/news/management/leaders-and-success/
john-paul-dejoria-rose-from-homelessness-to-king-of-hairstyling/.

Stillwell, Kate. 2018. "How This Entrepreneur Bounced Back After Losing A
Partnership, Laying Off Her Team And Dealing With $100 Million At Stake".
Entrepreneur. https://www.entrepreneur.com/article/324254.

"The Top 20 Reasons Startups Fail". 2018. *CB Insights Research*. https://www.
cbinsights.com/research/startup-failure-reasons-top/.

The Unofficial Stanford Blog. 2008. "Iinnovate Presents Barry Mccarthy, Chief
Financial Officer Of Netflix". Podcast.

CHAPTER 3 - THE BRAIN:

Dweck, Carol S. 2015. "Growth Mindset, Revisited". *Education Week*, , 2015.
http://ew.edweek.org/nxtbooks/epe/ew_09232015/index.php?startid=24#/24.

Dweck, Carol S. 2008. "Mindsets And Math/Science Achievement". http://www.
growthmindsetmaths.com/uploads/2/3/7/7/23776169/mindset_and_math_sci-
ence_achievement_-_nov_2013.pdf.

Fuchs, Eberhard, and Gabriele Flügge. 2014. "Adult Neuroplasticity: More Than
40 Years Of Research". *Neural Plasticity*, 1-10. doi:10.1155/2014/541870.

Gladding, M.D., Rebecca. 2013. "This Is Your Brain On Meditation". *Psychology Today*. https://www.psychologytoday.com/us/blog/
use-your-mind-change-your-brain/201305/is-your-brain-meditation.

"Katieringley.Co". n.d. *Katieringley.Co*. https://katie-ringley.squarespace.com/
home/?offset=1530271904927.

Kurzweil, Raymond. 2000. *The Age Of Spiritual Machines*. New York: Pen-
guin Books.

"The Origins Of Language". 2013. *Arafatduogabriel.Blogspot.Com*. http://arafat-
duogabriel.blogspot.com/2013/05/the-origins-of-language.html.

"Split Brain Behavioral Experiments". 2007. *Youtube*. https://www.youtube.com/watch?v=ZMLzP1VCAN0.

Wolman, David. 2012. "The Split Brain: A Tale Of Two Halves". *Nature* 483 (7389): 260-263. doi:10.1038/483260a.

CHAPTER 4: THE INNOVATOR'S MINDSET:

Forrester Consulting. 2014. "The Creative Dividend: How Creativity Impacts Business Results". https://landing.adobe.com/dam/downloads/whitepapers/55563.en.creative-dividends.pdf.

Hilliam, Rachel. 2005. *Galileo Galilei: Father Of Modern Science*. New York: Rosen Pub. Group.

McMullin, Ernan. "Galileo and Peter Lombard." *History Ireland* 15, no. 4 (2007): 22-26. http://www.jstor.org/stable/27725654.

"The Top 20 Reasons Startups Fail". 2018. *CB Insights Research*. https://www.cbinsights.com/research/startup-failure-reasons-top/.

CHAPTER 5: HOW MEDITATION AFFECTS THE BRAIN

Chopra, Deepak. 2017. "Why Meditate?". *Deepakchopra.Com*. https://www.deepakchopra.com/blog/article/4701?sso_code=eyJpdiI6InJkdogyZFZrNnZpaW1ScooySEpZSGc9PSIsInZhbHVlIjoiTFJppNoVNSTRqYWlsWm5MNlk1Z29yZHFZWlVvVXFnR1ZOV3dSbzJtM3NhaUJzaUVVnclQrVoR1dohNN2U1WGJZMG1CclhNaCtmdU9ZaFY1TklJNG82NXJUXC92d1RZSW1qQjhWWaok3NTZDM2RNPSIsIm1hYyI6IjNmNGE4YmY5MjYyYjIoYmY5ZDM3ZWYwM2RhOTlkMTYyYTM2NjNiNDU2ZjY5Zj5OGQ2YjViWU0oOWJjOODY4MTQifQ%3D%3D.

David Lynch Foundation. 2013. *Jerry Seinfeld Talks Transcendental Meditation At David Lynch Foundation Gala*. Video. https://www.youtube.com/watch?v=uh7Yru3cHoA.

Kral, Tammi R.A., Brianna S. Schuyler, Jeanette A. Mumford, Melissa A. Rosenkranz, Antoine Lutz, and Richard J. Davidson. 2018. "Impact Of Short- And Long-Term Mindfulness Meditation Training On Amygdala Reactivity To Emotional Stimuli". *Neuroimage* 181: 301-313. doi:10.1016/j.neuroimage.2018.07.013.

Roth, Bob, and Raja Felix Kaegi. 2014. *Transcendental Meditation Technique - A Complete Introduction By Bob Roth*. Video. https://vimeo.com/87931619.

Schulte, Brigid. 2015. "Harvard Neuroscientist: Meditation Not Only Reduces Stress, Here'S How It Changes Your Brain". *The Washington Post*. https://www. washingtonpost.com/news/inspired-life/wp/2015/05/26/harvard-neuroscientist-meditation-not-only-reduces-stress-it-literally-changes-your-brain/?noredirect=on&utm_term=.2db613d7c260.

Spoon, Marianne. 2018. "Meditation Affects Brain Networks Differently In Long-Term Meditators And Novices". *News.Wisc.Edu*. https://news.wisc.edu/meditation-affects-brain-networks-differently-in-long-term-meditators-and-novices/.

CHAPTER 6: MIND-BODY CONNECTION

Chapman, Benjamin P., Kevin Fiscella, Ichiro Kawachi, Paul Duberstein, and Peter Muennig. 2013. "Emotion Suppression And Mortality Risk Over A 12-Year Follow-Up". *Journal Of Psychosomatic Research* 75 (4): 381-385. doi:10.1016/j.jpsychores.2013.07.014.

Goleman, Daniel. 1988. "Probing The Enigma Of Multiple Personality". *The New York Times*, , 1988. https://www.nytimes.com/1988/06/28/science/probing-the-enigma-of-multiple-personality.html.

Gough, William C. 1999. "THE CELLULAR COMMUNICATION PROCESS AND ALTERNATIVE MODES OF HEALING". *Subtle Energies And Energy Medicine: An Interdeiciplinary Journal Of Energetic & Informational Interactions* 8 (2).

History.com. 2011. *Tibetan Buddhist Monks Meditation And Science. Tummo Meditation*.. Video. https://www.youtube.com/watch?v=XZUdtFu_hwI.

Kox, M, LT van Eijk, J Zwaag, J van den Wildenberg, FCJG Sweep, JG van der Hoeven, and P Pickkers. 2014. "0026. Voluntary Activation Of The Sympathetic Nervous System And Attenuation Of The Innate Immune Response In Humans". *Intensive Care Medicine Experimental* 2 (Suppl 1): O2. doi:10.1186/2197-425x-2-s1-o2.

McCraty, Rollin, Ph.D. Mike Atkinson, and Dana Tomasino, B.A. 2003. "MODULATION OF DNA CONFORMATION BY HEART-FOCUSED INTENTION". *Institute Of Heartmath*3 (8). http://www.aipro.info/drive/File/224.pdf.

Radboud University Nijmegen Medical Centre. 2011. "Research on 'Iceman' Wim Hof suggests it may be possible to influence autonomic nervous system and immune response." ScienceDaily. www.sciencedaily.com/releases/2011/04/110422090203.htm.

VICE. 2015. *Inside The Superhuman World Of The Iceman*. Video. https://www.youtube.com/watch?v=VaMjhwFE1Zw.

CHAPTER 7: PLACEBO EFFECT

"Definition Of PLACEBO". 2019. *Merriam-Webster.Com*. https://www.merriam-webster.com/dictionary/placebo.

Dispenza, Dr. Joe. 2014. *You Are The Placebo*. 1st ed. Hay House, Inc.

Placebo Effect - Caffeine Experiment. 2012. Video. https://www.youtube.com/watch?v=8Ox8QpxltSY.

Talbot, Margaret. 2000. "The Placebo Prescription". *The New York Times Magazine*, , 2000.

CHAPTER 8: A FOUNDER'S MEDITATION

Gandhi, Mahatma. n.d. "A Quote By Mahatma Gandhi". *Goodreads.Com*. https://www.goodreads.com/quotes/50584-your-beliefs-become-your-thoughts-your-thoughts-become-your-words.

CHAPTER 9: DEVELOPING INTENTION

Błachnio, Agata, Aneta Przepiorka, and Igor Pantic. 2016. "Association Between Facebook Addiction, Self-Esteem And Life Satisfaction: A Cross-Sectional Study". *Computers In Human Behavior* 55: 701-705. doi:10.1016/j.chb.2015.10.026.

Losier, Michael J. 2007. *Law Of Attraction*. New York: Wellness Central.

Muller, F. Max. 2014. *The Dhammapada*. 1st ed. CreateSpace Independent Publishing Platform.

CHAPTER 10: ENHANCING CREATIVITY

Ding, Xiaoqian, Yi-Yuan Tang, Rongxiang Tang, and Michael I Posner. 2014. "Improving Creativity Performance By Short-Term Meditation". *Behavioral And Brain Functions* 10 (1): 9. doi:10.1186/1744-9081-10-9.

Forrester Consulting. 2014. "The Creative Dividend: How Creativity Impacts Business Results". https://landing.adobe.com/dam/downloads/whitepapers/55563.en.creative-dividends.pdf.

IBM. 2010. "IBM 2010 Global CEO Study: Creativity Selected As Most Crucial Factor For Future Success". https://www-03.ibm.com/press/us/en/pressrelease/31670.wss#resource.

Knappenberger, Brian. 2010. *Steve Jobs*. Video. Bloomberg.

Landry, Lauren. 2017. "The Importance Of Creativity In Business". *Northeastern University Graduate Programs*. https://www.northeastern.edu/graduate/blog/creativity-importance-in-business/.

Pagano, Robert R., and Lynn R. Frumkin. 1977. "The Effect Of Transcendental Meditation On Right Hemispheric Functioning". *Biofeedback And Self-Regulation* 2 (4): 407-415. doi:10.1007/bf00998625.

Tedx Talks. 2011. *Tedxtucson George Land The Failure Of Success*. Video. https://www.youtube.com/watch?v=ZfKMq-rYtnc.

CHAPTER 11: IMPROVING COGNITION

Barclay, Rachel. 2013. "Your Memory Is Unreliable, And It'S About To Get Worse". *Healthline*. https://www.healthline.com/health-news/mental-memory-is-unreliable-and-it-could-be-worse-091313#1.

Barr, Alistair. 2010. "Soros Among Firms That Made Money In 2008, 2009". *Marketwatch*. https://www.marketwatch.com/story/soros-among-firms-that-made-money-in-08-and-09-2010-01-13.

Clifford, Catherine. 2018. "Hedge Fund Billionaire Ray Dalio: Meditation Is 'The Single Most Important Reason' For My Success". *CNBC*. https://www.cnbc.com/2018/03/16/bridgewater-associates-ray-dalio-meditation-is-key-to-my-success.html.

Cranson, Robert W., David W. Orme-Johnson, Jayne Gackenbach, Michael C. Dillbeck, Christopher H. Jones, and Charles N. Alexander. 1991. "Transcendental Meditation And Improved Performance On Intelligence-Related Measures: A Longitudinal Study". *Personality And Individual Differences*12 (10): 1105-1116. doi:10.1016/0191-8869(91)90040-i.

David Lynch Foundation. 2012. *Meditation Improves Performance At Military University*. Video. https://www.youtube.com/watch?v=0IH0913lQe0&t=2s.

Dillbeck, Michael C. 1982. "Meditation And Flexibility Of Visual Perception And Verbal Problem Solving". *Memory & Cognition* 10 (3): 207-215. doi:10.3758/bf03197631.

EDHEC Business School. 2009. "Hedge Fund Performance In 2008". http://docs.edhec-risk.com/mrk/000000/Press/EDHEC_Publication_HF_Performance_in_2008.pdf.

Feloni, Richard. 2016. "The World's Largest Hedge Fund Reimburses Employees Half The Cost Of $1,000 Meditation Lessons". *Business Insider*. https://www.businessinsider.com/transcendental-meditation-bridgewater-associates-2016-11.

Mainemelis, Charalampos, Richard E. Boyatzis, and David A. Kolb. 2002. "Learning Styles And Adaptive Flexibility". *Management Learning* 33 (1): 5-33. doi:10.1177/1350507602331001.

Myers, Melissa. 2015. "Improving Military Resilience Through Mindfulness Training". *Www.Army.Mil*. https://www.army.mil/article/149615/improving_military_resilience_through_mindfulness_training.

Quach, Dianna, Kristen E. Jastrowski Mano, and Kristi Alexander. 2016. "A Randomized Controlled Trial Examining The Effect Of Mindfulness Meditation On Working Memory Capacity In Adolescents". *Journal Of Adolescent Health* 58 (5): 489-496. doi:10.1016/j.jadohealth.2015.09.024.

Ren, Jun, ZhiHui Huang, Jing Luo, GaoXia Wei, XiaoPing Ying, ZhiGuang Ding, YiBin Wu, and Fei Luo. 2011. "Meditation Promotes Insightful Problem-Solving By Keeping People In A Mindful And Alert Conscious State". *Science China Life Sciences* 54 (10): 961-965. doi:10.1007/s11427-011-4233-3.

CHAPTER 12: PERSEVERANCE

"A Quick Guide To SNAP Eligibility And Benefits". 2018. *Center On Budget And Policy Priorities.* https://www.cbpp.org/research/food-assistance/a-quick-guide-to-snap-eligibility-and-benefits.

Alibaba Group. 2017. *Jack Ma And Charlie Rose Gateway '17 Fireside Chat.* Video. https://www.youtube.com/watch?v=ohfA8Hcwvic.

Alibaba Group. 2015. *Jack Ma Davos Interview On Jan. 23 2015.* Video. https://www.youtube.com/watch?v=aqSkQye85OQ.

CNBC Prime. 2018. *Shark Tank: From Waitress To Real Estate Mogul: Barbara Corcoran's Rise To Riches | CNBC Prime.* Video. https://www.youtube.com/watch?v=hvWyvDpV7jk.

Curtin, Melanie. 2019. "33 Steve Jobs Quotes That Will Inspire You To Success". *Inc.Com.* https://www.inc.com/melanie-curtin/33-steve-jobs-quotes-that-will-inspire-you-to-achieve-massive-success.html.

Eng, Dinah. 2019. "Barbara Corcoran - From Waitress To Real Estate Queen". *Fortune.* http://fortune.com/2013/05/23/barbara-corcoran-from-waitress-to-real-estate-queen/.

Eternal Explorer. 2019. *'GREATEST SUCCESS STORY' (Ft.Jack Ma) - Motivational Video | Jack Ma Speech | Inspirational Video.* Video. https://www.youtube.com/watch?v=KqJs_NHjV14.

CHAPTER 13: FAILURE

Allen, Paul. 2011. "My Favorite Mistake: Paul Allen". *Newsweek.* https://www.newsweek.com/my-favorite-mistake-paul-allen-66489.

Amason, Allen C., and Harry J. Sapienza. 1997. "The Effects Of Top Management Team Size And Interaction Norms On Cognitive And Affective Conflict". *Journal Of Management* 23 (4): 495-516. doi:10.1177/014920639702300401.

Business Insider. 2018. *Ray Dalio On The Next Financial Crisis, How He Started His Own Hedge Fund, Transparency At Work, And More.* Video. https://www.businessinsider.com/ray-dalio-bridgewater-associates-hedge-fund-financial-crisis-ignition-2018-12.

Chin, Kara. 2017. "Investing Legend Ray Dalio Shares The Simple Formula At The Heart Of His Success". *Business Insider*. https://www.businessinsider.com/bridgewater-ceo-ray-dalio-learning-from-mistakes-pain-reflection-progress-2017-5.

Hiskey, Davin. 2015. "The Shocking Story Behind Playdoh's Original Purpose". *Business Insider*. https://www.businessinsider.com/the-shocking-story-behind-playdohs-original-purpose-2015-9.

Mansfield, Matt. 2019. "STARTUP STATISTICS – The Numbers You Need To Know - Small Business Trends". *Small Business Trends*. https://smallbiztrends.com/2019/03/startup-statistics-small-business.html.

Weiss, Leah. 2018. "You Can't 'Fail Better' If You Don't Reflect On What You Learned". *Entrepreneur*. https://www.entrepreneur.com/article/310182.

CHAPTER 14: ENERGY LEVELS

Berger, Sarah. 2018. "Kevin O'leary: If You Want To Get Rich, Start Working 25 Hours A Day, 7 Days A Week". *CNBC*. https://www.cnbc.com/2018/11/14/kevin-oleary-says-entrepreneurs-work-25-hours-a-day-7-days-a-week.html.

David Lynch Foundation. 2015. *Martin Scorsese & Ray Dalio On Creativity, TM & Success | Highlights | David Lynch Foundation*. Video. https://www.youtube.com/watch?v=5-kJvsQh8Ak.

David Lynch Foundation. 2011. *Martin Scorsese On Transcendental Meditation And The David Lynch Foundation*. Video. https://www.youtube.com/watch?v=2Ic-ioVxyGA.

Harte, Jane L., Georg H. Eifert, and Roger Smith. 1995. "The Effects Of Running And Meditation On Beta-Endorphin, Corticotropin-Releasing Hormone And Cortisol In Plasma, And On Mood". *Biological Psychology* 40 (3): 251-265. doi:10.1016/0301-0511(95)05118-t.

Kaul, Prashant, Jason Passafiume, Craig R Sargent, and Bruce F O'Hara. 2010. "Meditation Acutely Improves Psychomotor Vigilance, And May Decrease Sleep Need". *Behavioral And Brain Functions* 6: 47. doi:10.1186/1744-9081-6-47.

Lennon, John, and George Harrison. 1967. Interview with John Lennon and George HarrisonDavid Frost Interview by . Radio. The Frost Programme.

Lennon, John, Paul McCartney, George Harrison, and Ringo Starr. 2000. *The Beatles Anthology*. 1st ed. Chronicle Books.

Roth, Bob, and Raja Felix Kaegi. 2014. *Transcendental Meditation Technique - A Complete Introduction By Bob Roth*. Video. https://vimeo.com/87931619.

"The Top 20 Reasons Startups Fail". 2018. *CB Insights Research*. https://www.cbinsights.com/research/startup-failure-reasons-top/.

CHAPTER 15: LONG GAME:

Bloomberg. 2014. "Masters In Business: Dallas Mavericks Mark Cuban". Podcast. *Bloomberg Opinion*. https://soundcloud.com/bloombergview/masters-in-business-dallas.

"Edison's Lightbulb". 2018. *The Franklin Institute*. https://www.fi.edu/history-resources/edisons-lightbulb.

Gladwell, Malcolm. 2009. *Outliers*. New York: Back Bay Books/Little, Brown.

Mansfield, Matt. 2019. "STARTUP STATISTICS – The Numbers You Need To Know - Small Business Trends". *Small Business Trends*. https://smallbiztrends.com/2019/03/startup-statistics-small-business.html.

Martin, Bobby. 2017. *The Hockey Stick Principles*. Flatiron Books.

Montag, Ali. 2018. "Mark Cuban Says This Side Hustle As A 12-Year-Old Taught Him 'As Much About Business As Any Class'". *CNBC*. https://www.cnbc.com/2018/08/10/what-mark-cubans-childhood-side-hustle-taught-him-about-business.html.

CHAPTER 16: WELL-BEING

Brand, Russell. 2017. *Recovery: Freedom From Our Addictions*. Henry Holt and Co.

Blynn, Jamie. 2017. "Russell Brand Candidly Opens Up About His Heroin, Sex Addiction And His Marriage To Katy Perry". *US Weekly*. https://www.usmagazine.com/celebrity-news/news/russell-brand-on-heroin-sex-addiction-and-katy-perry-w507520/.

David Lynch Foundation. 2011. *Russell Brand Talks About Transcendental Meditation At Operation Warrior Wellness Launch.* Video. https://www.youtube.com/watch?v=zTG4UcxR_8M.

Foley, Benjamin. 2017. "Suicide, Entrepreneurship, And The Road Home". *Medium.* https://medium.com/startup-grind/how-trying-to-be-somebody-almost-killed-me-and-the-9-steps-i-took-to-get-my-life-back-77348a598a32.

Keune, Philipp M., and Dóra Perczel Forintos. 2010. "Mindfulness Meditation: A Preliminary Study On Meditation Practice During Everyday Life Activities And Its Association With Well-Being". *Psychological Topics*, 373-386.

Ruby, Jennifer. 2015. "Fifi Geldof Slams Russell Brand For 'Inappropriate' Drugs Joke At". *Evening Standard.* https://www.standard.co.uk/showbiz/celebrity-news/fifi-geldof-slams-russell-brand-for-inappropriate-drugs-joke-at-fundraiser-following-sister-peaches-10347018.html.

Sinha, Rajita. 2011. "New Findings On Biological Factors Predicting Addiction Relapse Vulnerability". *Current Psychiatry Reports* 13 (5): 398-405. doi:10.1007/s11920-011-0224-0.

TODAY. 2017. *Russell Brand On Recovery From Addiction And His 'Villainous' Baby Daughter | Megyn Kelly TODAY.* Video. https://www.youtube.com/watch?v=WU_Bbaki3fo.

CONCLUSION:

Koester, Eric. 2018. "Bonus: What's On Alec Ross's Nightstand?". Podcast. *The Eric Koester Creator Institute.*

www.ingramcontent.com/pod-product-compliance
Lightning Source LLC
Chambersburg PA
CBHW071522180526
45171CB00002B/345